Building a Home Security
System with BeagleBone

Build your own high-tech alarm system at a fraction of
the cost

Bill Pretty

BIRMINGHAM - MUMBAI

Building a Home Security System with BeagleBone

First published: December 2013

Production Reference: 1101213

Published by Packt Publishing Ltd.

Livery Place
35 Livery Street
Birmingham B3 2PB, UK.

ISBN 978-1-78355-960-2

www.packtpub.com

Cover Image by Bill Pretty (Bill.pretty@xplornet.com)

Credits

Author
Bill Pretty

Reviewers
Toni de la Fuente (Blyx)
Naoya Hashimoto
Jaime Soriano Pastor
Norbert Varga
Kelli Waxman

Acquisition Editor
Sam Birch

Commissioning Editor
Amit Ghodake

Copy Editors
Roshni Banerjee
Mradula Hegde
Dipti Kapadia
Deepa Nambiar
Karuna Narayanan
Kirti Pai
Lavina Pereira

Technical Editors
Shubhangi Dhamgaye
Pratik More
Nachiket Vartak

Project Coordinator
Akash Poojary

Proofreader
Ting Baker

Indexer
Tejal Soni

Graphics
Ronak Dhruv
Abhinash Sahu

Production Coordinator
Adonia Jones

Cover Work
Adonia Jones

About the Author

Bill Pretty began his career in electronics in the early 80s with a small telecom startup company that eventually became a large multinational. He left there to pursue a career in commercial aviation in North Canada. From there he joined the Ontario Center for Microelectronics, a provincially funded research and development center. He left there for a career in the military as a civilian contractor at what was then called the Defense Research Establishment, Ottawa. That began a career that was to span the next 25 years, and continues today.

Over the years, Bill has acquired extensive knowledge in the field of technical security and started his own company in 2010. That company is called William Pretty Security Inc. and provides support in the form of research and development to various law enforcement and private security agencies.

While this is Bill's first book, he has published and presented a number of white papers on the subject of technical security. Bill was also a guest presenter for a number of years at the Western Canada Technical Conference, a law-enforcement-only conference held every year in Western Canada. A selection of these papers is available for download on his website.

There are a number of people I would like to thank, for without their support this book would never have been started. My good friends Peter, Sam, Carol, Will, and Kelli for believing in me even when I didn't. To my life partner, Donna, who never stopped believing. And last but not least, my good friend and fellow code warrior Willie, the Mad Scott.

About the Reviewers

Toni de la Fuente is a Senior Solutions Engineer for Americas at Alfresco Software Inc. The highlight of his career is the more-than-14 years' experience he has in Systems Administration, Networking, and Security. He also has the LPI Linux and ITIL v3 certifications and is a Red Hat Certified Engineer (RHCE); recently, he has been certified as a AWS Technical Professional and AWS Business Professional.

He is an open source enthusiast, having founded different open source projects in previous years. He has participated in other open-source-related projects, such as Madrid Wireless, Fedora Linux, and OpenSolaris Hispano, and been referenced in books on network security. He is into teaching and regularly takes lectures, courses, and conferences at different events in Europe, the United States, and Latin America. He has also been contributing to the world of open source for more than 10 years with his blog http://blyx.com and through Twitter (@ToniBlyx).

> I want to say thanks to Packt Publishing for their trust in me and to all the people who have spent tons of hours working at night making open source—you all make this world a better place, keep going.

Naoya Hashimoto has been working on Linux system integration and system and operation maintenance, both on premises and public cloud, for years. He has experience in planning, designing, and developing a new service to manage, maintain, and monitor a system on public cloud for 1-2 years in Japan.

His company is going to release a new service called Grow Cloud to manage, maintain, and monitor a system on Amazon Web Services this fall or winter in Japan. The customer support center supports Chinese, English, and Japanese. You can contact Naoya without hesitation if you have any question or are interested in our new service.

He has worked on books such as *Icinga Network Monitoring* and *OSS DB Standard Text – PostgreSQL* (`http://www.oss-db.jp/ossdbtext/text.shtml`) and was also involved in the translation of some chapters from Japanese to English.

Thanks to Amit Ghodake, Akash Poojary, Vineeta Darade, and Amigya Khurana for giving me the opportunity to review *Chapter 7, Protecting Your Network*, of *Building a Home Security System with BeagleBone*, which was the second time to review technical books, the first time was *Icinga Network Monitoring*. I wouldn't have had the experience to review this book without my work with Icinga. Lastly, I'd like to express my gratitude to Forschooner, Inc. as they have given me the opportunity to publish a company blog about OSS system integration and maintenance, mainly in Japanese and a few in English.

Jaime Soriano Pastor was born in Teruel, a small city in Spain. He has always been passionate about technology and sciences. While studying Computer Science at the university in his hometown, he had his first contact with Linux and free software, which has deeply influenced his career. Later on, he moved to Zaragoza to continue his studies and there he worked for a couple of companies on quite different and interesting projects, from operative systems in embedded devices to the cloud, giving him a wide view of several fields of software development as well as opportunities to travel around Europe. He currently lives in Madrid. Configuration management and continuous integration form part of his daily work as a tools engineer in a well-known Internet company.

Norbert Varga has over four years of experience in the software and hardware development industry. He is responsible for embedded software development, hardware-software integration, and wireless telecommunication solutions at his current employer, BME-Infokom.

He has extensive experience in networking and hardware-software integration and has engineered advanced systems, including wireless mesh networks and smart metering solutions. He also has a strong background in Linux system administration and software development.

Previously, Norbert worked as a software developer on various projects at the Budapest University of Technology and Economics (Department of Telecommunications), which is the most renowned technical university in Hungary. Norbert played a key role throughout all the development processes, ranging from initial planning through implementation to testing and production support.

Kelli Waxman is a high-tech crime investigator, adjunct faculty for Texas A&M TEEX, instructor at Homeland Security Defense Coalition, and President of National Security Consulting & Investigations PLLC. Kelli's background includes being a sociologist, criminolgist, MBA, private investigator, and former 100-mile endurance horse racer. She is an avid Grand Canyon hiker and advanced classical pianist. She is a US government contractor.

I'd like to thank Bill and Packt Publishing for being patient with us in returning the reviews. We were in the middle of major upgrades and migrations, as well as beta testing some products. Our engineers reminded us that their brains were tired.

www.PacktPub.com

Support files, eBooks, discount offers and more

You might want to visit www.PacktPub.com for support files and downloads related to your book.

Did you know that Packt offers eBook versions of every book published, with PDF and ePub files available? You can upgrade to the eBook version at www.PacktPub.com and as a print book customer, you are entitled to a discount on the eBook copy. Get in touch with us at service@packtpub.com for more details.

At www.PacktPub.com, you can also read a collection of free technical articles, sign up for a range of free newsletters and receive exclusive discounts and offers on Packt books and eBooks.

http://PacktLib.PacktPub.com

Do you need instant solutions to your IT questions? PacktLib is Packt's online digital book library. Here, you can access, read and search across Packt's entire library of books.

Why Subscribe?

- Fully searchable across every book published by Packt
- Copy and paste, print and bookmark content
- On demand and accessible via web browser

Free Access for Packt account holders

If you have an account with Packt at www.PacktPub.com, you can use this to access PacktLib today and view nine entirely free books. Simply use your login credentials for immediate access.

This book is dedicated to anyone who has ever fallen down and had the courage to get back up.

In the words of Albert Einstein, "Anyone who has never failed, has never tried anything new."

Table of Contents

Preface

I have been in the security industry for over 25 years, in one capacity or another, and there is something I would like to share with you.

One of the best kept secrets of the security and access control industry is just how simple the monitoring hardware actually is. It is the software that runs on the monitoring hardware that makes it seem cool.

The original BeagleBone, or the new BeagleBone Black, has all the computing power that you need to build yourself an extremely sophisticated access control, alarm panel, home automation, and network-intrusion-detection system.

All for less than a year's worth of monitoring charges from your local alarm company!

While we are on the topic of monitored alarm systems, there is no such thing as a FREE alarm system. It is like a free lunch. Where I come from, I can buy and install a basic home alarm system for less than $500.00. But if you sign up for a "free" system, monthly monitoring fees will be between $20 and $25 per month. So, in just over a year and a half, I have paid for my "free" alarm system. Most alarm companies will sign you for a three-year contract, but for (36 x $25) $900, you can build yourself one heck of an alarm system, plus one for your buddy too!

Don't get me wrong, monitored alarm systems have their place, for example, your elderly mother or your convenience store in a bad part of the town. There is no substitute for a live human on the other end of the line.

That said, if you are reading this, you are probably a builder or a hobbyist with all the skills required to do it yourself.

If you have a friend or a relative who is a good carpenter, you have got it made. They will be an indispensible part of your team when it comes to installation.

This book will show you how to build and program your own high-tech alarm and home automation system. By the end of the book, you will have a basic knowledge of how alarm systems work and you will have built and tested your own basic alarm system.

The only limit will be your imagination.

So, let's get started!

What this book covers

Chapter 1, *Alarm Systems 101*, explains what the major components of an alarm system are and what they do.

Chapter 2, *Our Very First Alarm System*, covers how to build our first alarm system on a breadboard.

Chapter 3, *Bigger and Better*, covers what to build depending on what you've learned in the previous chapter, and thus make your system even better.

Chapter 4, *Building the Hardware*, covers how you build the actual hardware that your BeagleBone will use to connect to an external source.

Chapter 5, *Testing the Hardware*, covers how you test the hardware that you've built. This is where the rubber meets the road. Does your creation work?

Chapter 6, *Automating Stuff*, introduces some additional uses of the alarm system hardware. Now that you have a working system, it is time to do other things than just monitor some switches.

Chapter 7, *Protecting Your Network*, covers how you will be moving even further away from the conventional alarm system by using the BeagleBone to monitor the status of your home network. Here, you give the BeagleBone something to do in its spare time, such as protecting your network from the bad guys.

Chapter 8, *Keeping an Eye on Things*, covers how you can keep an eye on things while away from home. Sitting in a café in Paris and want to know how things are going back home? This chapter shows how to do it.

Chapter 9, *Going Further*, covers some of the many more cool things you can do with your system. Now that you have all this great new knowledge and a cool platform to play with, you are limited (almost) only by your imagination. Just to get you started, I have added a few suggestions.

What you need for this book

What you need for this book depends largely on what your interest in alarm and security systems is.

If it is a general interest, then all you need is this book. You will find that there is very little technical jargon, and that what there is, is explained as simply as I can.

If you are a programmer who wants to get your feet wet when it comes to hardware, then this book is for you too. If you are an advanced programmer, you may find the code a bit simplistic. What can I say, I'm a hardware guy!

If you are a hardware guy like me and a builder–tinkerer, you will love this book. There is enough software provided to keep you out of trouble for the most part.

But what you need most of all for this book is an insatiable curiosity!

Who this book is for

The title of this book suggests that it is only for BeagleBone owners. In fact, the hardware is designed in such a way that it will work with any single-board computer with I/O capability. So if you are a Raspberry Pi, Arduino, or Gumstix owner, don't be put off.

This book is for you too. You will have to write your own software, but we will provide all the source code.

This book is also for anyone who is interested in alarm systems and how they work. It is also for hobbyists and basement tinkerers who love to build things.

As for skills, if you want to build the hardware, you will need some basic soldering skills. All the parts are through-hole variety, so basic skills are all that is required.

When it comes to software, you can just run it as it is. If you want to modify code, then you will require knowledge of Java and integrated development environments.

We will also have a working 4 GB image file that you can download and burn onto a USD card, and be up and running in minutes.

Conventions

In this book, you will find a number of styles of text that distinguish between different kinds of information. Here are some examples of these styles, and an explanation of their meaning.

Code words in text are shown as follows: "You can access the Cloud9 integrated development environment (IDE) from the `Start.html` link on the microSD card image."

A block of code is set as follows:

```
<html>
  <head>
    <title>Wireless Hub Access Page</title>
  </head>
  <body>
  <h1>Here is a simple way of accessing your Router via
  Yaler:</h1>


    <a href="http:192.168.10.1"> Here is my Router Page </a>

  </body>
</html>
```

When we wish to draw your attention to a particular part of a code block, the relevant lines or items are set in bold:

```
var outputPin1 = "P8_13";        //Alarm Output 1
var outputPin2 = 'P8_11';        //Alarm Output 2
var outputPin3 = 'P8_12';        //Alarm Output 3
var outputPin4 = 'P8_14';        //Alarm Output 4
```

Any command-line input or output is written as follows:

```
$ mkdir yalertunnel
$ cd yalertunnel
```

New terms and **important words** are shown in bold. Words that you see on the screen, in menus or dialog boxes for example, appear in the text like this: "Navigate to **Connection** | **Data** and set **Auto-login username** to `root`."

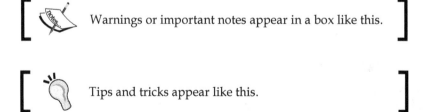

[Warnings or important notes appear in a box like this.]

[Tips and tricks appear like this.]

Reader feedback

Feedback from our readers is always welcome. Let us know what you think about this book—what you liked or may have disliked. Reader feedback is important for us to develop titles that you really get the most out of.

To send us general feedback, simply send an e-mail to feedback@packtpub.com, and mention the book title via the subject of your message.

If there is a topic that you have expertise in and you are interested in either writing or contributing to a book, see our author guide on www.packtpub.com/authors.

Customer support

Now that you are the proud owner of a Packt book, we have a number of things to help you to get the most from your purchase.

Downloading the example code and image files

You can download the example code and image files for all Packt books you have purchased from your account at http://www.packtpub.com. If you purchased this book elsewhere, you can visit http://www.packtpub.com/support and register to have the files e-mailed directly to you.

Errata

Although we have taken every care to ensure the accuracy of our content, mistakes do happen. If you find a mistake in one of our books—maybe a mistake in the text or the code—we would be grateful if you would report this to us. By doing so, you can save other readers from frustration and help us improve subsequent versions of this book. If you find any errata, please report them by visiting http://www.packtpub.com/submit-errata, selecting your book, clicking on the **errata submission form** link, and entering the details of your errata. Once your errata are verified, your submission will be accepted and the errata will be uploaded on our website, or added to any list of existing errata, under the Errata section of that title. Any existing errata can be viewed by selecting your title from http://www.packtpub.com/support.

Piracy

Piracy of copyright material on the Internet is an ongoing problem across all media. At Packt, we take the protection of our copyright and licenses very seriously. If you come across any illegal copies of our works, in any form, on the Internet, please provide us with the location address or website name immediately so that we can pursue a remedy.

Please contact us at `copyright@packtpub.com` with a link to the suspected pirated material.

We appreciate your help in protecting our authors, and our ability to bring you valuable content.

Questions

You can contact us at `questions@packtpub.com` if you are having a problem with any aspect of the book, and we will do our best to address it.

1
Alarm Systems 101

In this chapter, we will cover the major components that almost all alarm systems have in common. By the end of the chapter you will realize that the so-called high tech alarm systems and access control systems are not really as complicated as some would like you to believe.

That said, let's get started.

Every alarm system in the world does two and only two basic things.

- It monitors the world around it. If the alarm is your neighbor's dog, it keeps an eye on trespassers. If it is an alarm system, then the central control panel monitors a bank of contacts (switches) and waits for something to change (just like the dog). These contacts are the output parts of various kinds of sensors. This is how the sensor tells the panel that something has changed. There are many kinds of sensors, about which I will tell you shortly, but they all signal the panel in much the same way.

- When the panel detects a change, it takes an appropriate action based on what the change was. It could be an alarm condition, or it could be a proper access control request. To use the dog scenario again, it could be you coming home from work, in which case the dog wags its tail. It could be the mailman, a bill collector, a burglar, or someone the dog doesn't know. In this case we have an *alarm* condition and the dog does its thing!

Cool facts

It doesn't matter if it is the Bank of England or your cottage in Kent, the only major difference is how sophisticated (expensive) the sensors are and how fancy (expensive) the monitoring software is!

Also, I'm sure many of you have seen Tom Cruise drop from the ceiling to avoid the laser grid in Mission Impossible. You could have caught him with a $20 PIR motion sensor and saved yourself the price of the fancy lasers!

In my experience, you don't have to be an electrical engineer to install an alarm system, just a good carpenter, painter, and plasterer! By the way, I'm not, so I'll leave it up to you to hide the wires.

Also, because our alarm system runs on 12 volts, you don't have to be a licensed electrician to install it. If you can plug in a "wall wart" you are there! Fascinated yet? Read on....

And now, more on sensors and how they work.

Door and window switches

The first sensor we will talk about is the door/window contact switch. This is by far the most common type of sensor used in the alarm industry. There are several variations of this sensor, but they all function in the same way. For example, you can buy a garage door sensor that has a large magnet and is physically large, so that when the wind sways your garage door, the rattling won't set off the alarm.

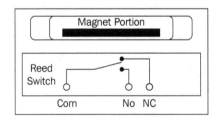

Typical door or window contacts

The preceding diagram shows a standard door or window sensor. Usually the contact position is when the reed switch is energized (the window is closed). If you aren't sure, check with an ohm meter.

The magnet normally holds the wiper of the reed switch against the normally closed contact. When the window or door is opened, the magnet can no longer hold the wiper against the normally closed contact and it opens.

You can think of a sensor as a magnetically operated single pole double throw (SPDT) switch. In fact, for testing purposes, you can use a toggle switch to simulate door and window contacts.

Remember what I said about carpentry?

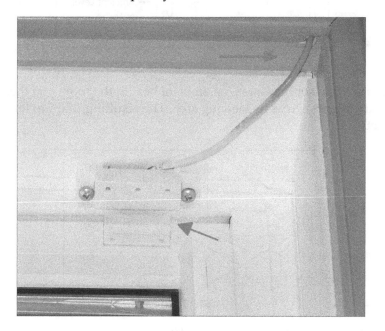

Installed window contacts

The preceding photograph is of an actual installation. The magnet (bottom arrow) is installed on the window, while the switch is on the window frame. The top arrow shows a poor installation job! The installer should have drilled a hole in the window frame closer to the switch, so that not much of the wire is exposed. The less exposed wire there is, the harder it is for the bad guys to bypass the switch. The same rule applies to all types of sensor installations.

The PIR – passive infrared sensor

The next most common sensor is the passive infrared motion sensor or PIR.

It is called a passive infrared sensor because it does not transmit anything. If, for example, it used an IR laser, it would be an active sensor. PIRs come in many shapes, sizes, and price ranges. Many of the more expensive models can be configured so that the family pet does not activate the sensor.

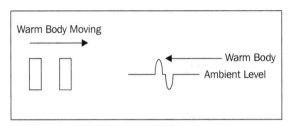

PIR motion sensing

A passive infrared sensor measures the ambient heat in the room and then waits for a warmer body to pass across its viewing area. The resulting "blip" in the ambience is what it detects.

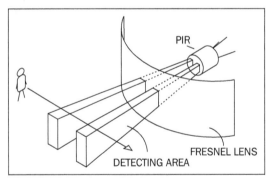

Fresnel lens

A Fresnel lens and a parabolic mirror are often used to extend the range of the sensor. Think of it as a flashlight in reverse. Instead of concentrating the light from the bulb into a beam, the ambient IR focuses on the sensor. In the preceding diagram, the mirror would be behind the Fresnel lens. The Fresnel lens acts like a camera lens to give the sensor a wider field of view. This is an extremely simplified explanation. Modern PIRs use digital signal processing to help eliminate false triggering. All you need to worry about is the field of view of the PIR, because that is what you will use when you install your PIRs. Most PIRs have about a 90 or 120 degree field of view. It is also possible to buy a PIR with a 360 degree field of view. This device looks like a dome, and mounts in the center of the room on the ceiling.

No matter how fancy the innards, in the end the result is a pair of contacts for your panel to read.

Glass break sensors

The next type of sensor that should be of interest to the reader is the glass break detector. This detector replaces the foil tape that you may have seen on the front windows of many stores. This tape was a pain to apply properly and depending on the climate, could dry out and crack.

Modern glass break detectors use a microphone, an amplifier, and digital signal processing to detect breaking glass.

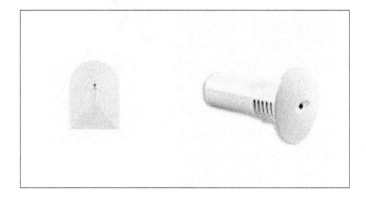

Typical glass break sensors

The sound of breaking glass is picked up by the microphone, amplified, and then filtered and detected by the software of the sensor.

Once again, the result is a set of contacts that open and close to indicate an alarm to your panel.

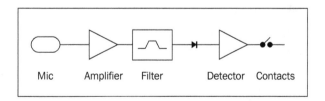

Glass break sensor block diagram

The temperature rise sensor

The final sensor of interest is the temperature rise sensor. This sensor is replacing the ionization type smoke detector in many modern buildings. Unlike a cheap ionization type of smoke detector, burning toast won't set it off! Much like the PIR and the glass break detector, it uses digital signal processing to sense a rapid rise in the ambient temperature, which would indicate a fire.

Also like the other detectors, it signals the panel by opening and closing a set of contacts.

Heat rise sensor

Summary

In this chapter we covered the four most common sensors found in the average home or small business areas, and briefly discussed how they work. These sensors, with the exception of door contacts, come in all different shapes, sizes, and models.

For example, there are a number of different models of PIRs. Some are "pet tolerant", meaning that a dog or cat won't set them off in the middle of the night.

Cool fact

Well, maybe not exactly a fact, but I've been told that in tropical climates, small lizards crawling across a PIR have set it off. I suppose that a gecko up close to the sensor looks like Godzilla!

In the next chapter we will be learning the theory behind our first alarm system. We will also be writing some simple code to simulate a one-zone alarm system, using the built-in IDE of BeagleBone.

Our Very First Alarm System

2

In this chapter we are going to design a single zone alarm system and learn how the basic components work. We will learn about comparators and how they are used in this case. We will also build and test a simple breadboard circuit that will simulate a single zone alarm. For example, the bell that rings when you enter a store.

Zones

A zone is an area that is being protected, and/or a collection of sensors that are protecting the zone. Zones can contain Passive Infrared Sensors (PIR sensors), glass break detectors, window contacts, or a combination of different sensors.

For example, "ground floor windows" could be a zone. Ground floor PIR sensors could be another zone. There are also "special" zones such as fire alarm zones. In commercial installations, the fire alarm zones and CO (carbon monoxide) detectors must have their own zone.

In the following chapters, you will see how we will use these zones to create a layered defense.

The hardware

The alarm system, in this case the BeagleBone, must be able to monitor the world around it. It does this by using ICs called comparators. You can think of a comparator as an op-amp with extremely high gain. Like an op-amp, when the voltage on the positive (+) input is higher than the voltage on the negative (-) input, the output goes high. When the opposite is true, the output goes low.

The LM339 comparator

We will be using an LM339 comparator. I chose the LM339 comparator because it has been around forever, and still comes in through-hole DIP packages. It is cheap and easy to source. Best of all, it is hard to blow up! The device has an open collector output. What this means is, a resistor is required to pull the output high. By connecting the output pull-up resistor to 3.3V, we now have a level converter that can be safely connected to the BeagleBone.

In the following diagram of the single zone comparator circuit, a 4.7K ohm resistor — **R5** is used as a pull-up. The LM339 comparator can sink plenty of current; so for debugging purposes, we will also connect **D1** and **R6** to the output. That way when the comparator is triggered, D1 will turn on. The other handy feature of the open collector output is that you can connect them together without damaging the output. This is often called a logical OR.

References:

- Op-amp: http://en.wikipedia.org/wiki/Operational_amplifier

- Comparator: http://en.wikipedia.org/wiki/Comparator

- OR Gate: http://en.wikipedia.org/wiki/OR_gate

The following circuit diagram actually monitors for two different conditions. If condition 1 is true, then pin 2 goes low or if condition 2 is true, then pin 2 goes low.

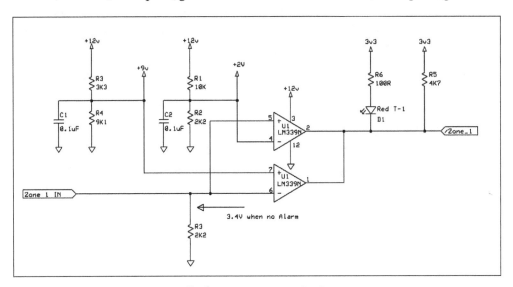

Single zone comparator circuit

The previous diagram is for one zone. In this project book, it is replicated four times for four zones. However, readers are free to replicate this circuit for as many zones as they have inputs on their BeagleBone.

The EOL – End Of Line resistor

An end of line resistor is a resistor that is installed in the last device (sensor) of a chain of devices; hence the term end of line resistor.

Resistors **R4**, **R3**, and the end of line resistor (marker EOL on the schematic) form a voltage divider. Basically, you have 5.6K and 2.2K in series and they are connected to 12V. Therefore, Ohm's law tells us that there will be about 3.4V at the plus input of the comparator when the alarm contacts are closed.

Resistors **R1** and **R2** form a voltage divider that provides a 2V reference for the negative input. As we learned before, if the plus input (3.4V) is higher than the minus input (2.0V), then the output will be high.

If the alarm condition occurs and the switch opens, then the 2.2K resistor, R3, will pull the input to 0V and the output will be low because the input is now less than 2.0V.

This also happens if the wire is cut by a burglar.

The following diagram shows what happens when the circuit is opened, either by an alarm contact or by a cut wire.

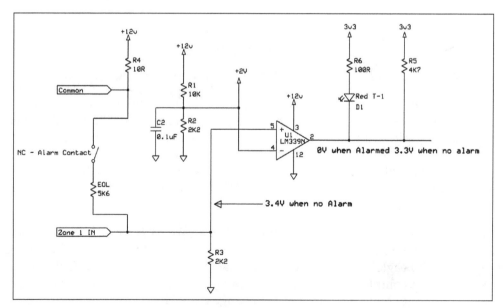

Open circuit condition

The following diagram shows what happens when someone or something shorts out the alarm contacts.

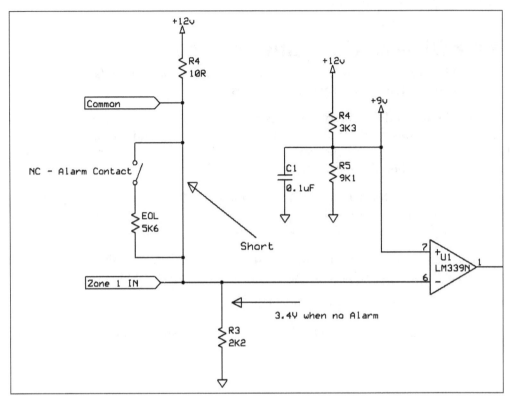

Contacts shorted

What if the burglar tries to jumper the alarm contacts and shorts out the EOL resistor?

In this case, the minus input of the LM339 comparator goes higher than the positive input, and once again the output is pulled low. Then, the reference voltage (9.0V) is applied to the positive input, and the sense voltage is applied to the minus input. If the EOL resistor is shorted, then 12V is applied to the minus input of the comparator, and the output is pulled low, once again. As we have learned before, the outputs of the two circuits are logically ORd together, so that if either an open circuit or a short circuit occurs, the alarm will be triggered.

I could have split the circuit into two different signals for each zone. One to indicate a short circuit, and one to indicate an open circuit. But, in order to reduce the number of inputs to the BeagleBone, I have connected the two outputs together. It also makes the software less complex. If you are a good programmer, you could use two inputs for each zone, but you would also have to change the PCB.

You may have also noticed that there is a considerable difference between the sense voltage and the reference voltage. This is to allow for long runs of wire, and for those of you who like to use Google. It is called hysteresis.

If you have a professionally installed alarm panel or know someone who does, open the panel and look at the terminal blocks where the wires are attached to the panel. If you see the resistors connected across the screw terminals with wires connected to them, the alarm system was NOT installed properly! What you do about this is up to you. The end of line resistors are called that for a reason! They belong at the END of the string of contacts. Installing them in the panel is a lazy way of doing things, and does nothing to protect the contacts from being bypassed.

The software

The programming language that I chose was JavaScript. This is because it is already well supported on the BeagleBone as it comes to you from the supplier. You can access the Cloud9 integrated development environment (IDE) from the `Start.html` link on the microSD card image.

There are plenty of very good tutorials and videos on how to use the Cloud9 IDE, so I have not included one here.

What the software does is, it watches an input pin waiting for it to go low. If the pin goes low, the software makes an output pin go high. This simulates an alarm panel monitoring a set of contacts, waiting for an alarm to occur.

In order to turn the alarm off, the software monitors another pin. If this pin goes low, it turns the alarm off. This is to simulate an alarm key switch being turned to the disarm position, but any type of contact closure will do.

Downloading the example code and image files

You can download the example code and image files for all Packt books you have purchased from your account at `http://www.packtpub.com`. If you purchased this book elsewhere, you can visit `http://www.packtpub.com/support` and register to have the files e-mailed directly to you.

We won't be building and testing the actual alarm system hardware until the following chapters, so for now, we will build ourselves an "alarm system simulator". In order to do that, I built the following circuit.

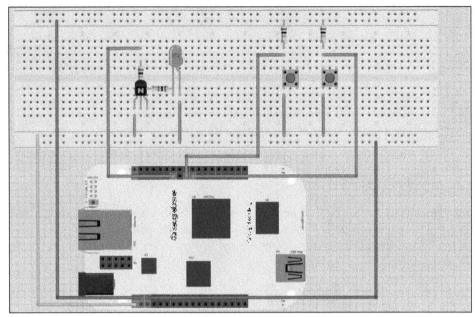

Breadboard layout

The following schematics will show in more detail how the circuit was constructed. The 3.3V power comes from the BeagleBone connector — P9 pin 3. The 5V power comes from P9 pin 5 and the ground is P9 pin 1.

As I said before, all that the alarm system does is monitor contacts and take the appropriate action. The system doesn't know or care what is "behind" the contacts. To make it easier for the reader to understand, I have labelled the switches — **Alarm In** to simulate door or window contacts, and **Alarm Reset** to simulate the alarm reset button or the switch.

In the following diagram, the BeagleBone connector number and pin numbers are indicated by the flags attached to the circuit drawing. For example, P8-13 in the simulated siren drawing means pin 13 of connector P8 on the BeagleBone.

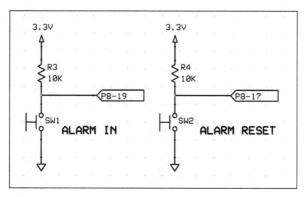

Simulated alarm contacts

In order to simulate an alarm bell or siren, I connected an LED to the alarm output pin. When the software detects an alarm, it will turn on the LED. We will be using a transistor on the outputs of the BeagleBone to boost the current capability of the output, and to hopefully protect the BeagleBone from external wiring errors. Note that the transistor also allows us to power the LED from 5V instead of 3.3V.

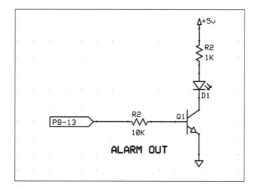

Simulated siren

Summary

In this chapter, we got our first introduction to the hardware and software that will be the heart of our alarm system.

We also learned how to stimulate the hardware using simple switches and an LED. We understood how comparators work and how to use them through this project. We briefly touched on EOL resistors and their significant use in this design.

In the next chapter, we will build the solid hardware that will be eventually connected to the BeagleBone.

3
Bigger and Better

In the previous chapter we built a simulated one zone alarm. Now we will learn how to install and wire basic sensors. Things such as window contacts, passive infrared sensors (PIRs), and glass break detectors. We will also learn about the most important part of any alarm system installation.

The planning phase

This is by far the most important part of the installation. Poor planning has caused more headaches than any other part of an alarm system installation project.

Step 1 – the walkabout

As the name suggests, take a walk around the property you will be protecting, both inside and outside. Try to think like a bad guy.

Ask yourself, "If I wanted to break into this house/office/warehouse, how would I do it?"

Take pictures if you think it will help. Make sketches of the inside and outside of the building, so that you can plan where you are going to put your sensors. There are a number of free landscaping **CAD** programs that will help you with this.

Here is a simple checklist for you:

- How many doors are there?
- What type of doors are they? Garage doors? Human entry doors? Pet doors? (Seriously, burglars have used children.)
- How many windows are there? How many open?
- How many windows are there on the ground floor and how many on the second floor? (Burglars use portable ladders.)

- Is there a hedge or a privacy fence? (Burglars love cedar hedges and privacy fences.)
- Once the burglar is inside, where can they go from there? (Main hallway, kitchen door, or patio door.)
- How many rooms are there that you will have to protect?
- Is everything on the same floor or is there more than one floor?
- What about special alarms? Panic alarm in the bedroom? Smoke alarm in the kitchen? Flood alarm in the basement?
- Hopefully, I have given you plenty to think about and we can now move on to step 2.

Your dream home

For the sake of this book we are going to protect your dream home. You just inherited a fortune from your long lost auntie, and you don't want the bad guys making off with your new found wealth.

The first floor

The following diagram depicts the first floor of your dream home:

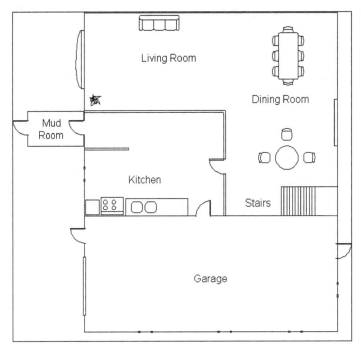

First floor

From your walkabout you noted that:

- There are two entrance doors with a mud room in between.
- There is a patio door off the dining room.
- The garage has two entry doors plus a large garage door.
- There is an entry door from the garage into the kitchen.
- The garage also has four windows, three on the side and one at the back.
- There is a kitchen window and a large bay window in the living room.
- Stairs lead up to the second floor, which has a landing at the top.

The second floor

The following diagram depicts the second floor of your dream home:

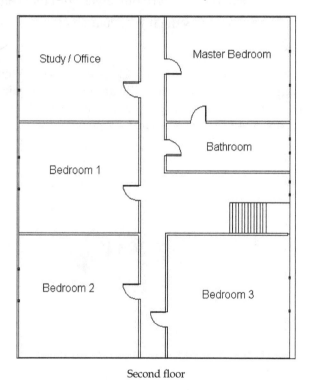

Second floor

From your walkabout you noted that:

- There is the main hallway off the second floor landing.
- All of the bedrooms and the study are accessed from this main hallway.
- Each of the bedrooms and the study has a window.

- There is also a window beside the second floor landing and in the bathroom.
- The bathroom is accessible from either the hallway or the master bedroom.
- Now that we have all this information carefully gathered, it is time to start planning our defenses in earnest.

We are going to employ what the military calls a layered-defense technique. It is exactly what it sounds like.

Step 2 – the layered-defense technique

So here is what we are going to do:

- We are going to plan a layered defense that uses different kinds of sensors.
- For this chapter we will only concern ourselves with the inside of the house.
- The exterior will be covered in the future chapters.
- Let's start with the garage.

Our first layer will be the doors and windows. There are three personal doors on which we can use simple magnetic switches. The garage door requires a special type of magnetic switch because garage doors tend to move too much and would cause false alarms if we used a small magnetic sensor.

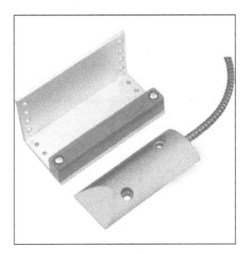

Magnetic garage door sensor

The next layer will be the motion sensors. In this case I would install a PIR sensor in the lower right-hand side of the garage. This way it can monitor all three doors plus the windows.

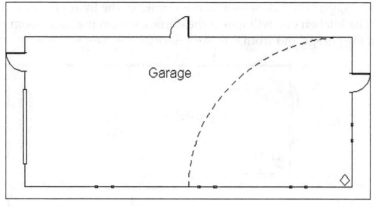

Garage PIR protection

Now that we have the garage protected, it is time to look at the rest of the bottom floor. Once again we will use a layered approach, by first protecting the door and windows. You will notice that the house has a vestibule or mud room as they are sometimes called. This is a good place to put a key switch that turns off the alarm. There is also hardware support for a second key switch, so you might want to install one by the kitchen door to the garage.

The outside door and inside door can be protected with standard magnetic door switches. As part of our layered-defense strategy, I would also put a door sensor on the door leading from the kitchen to the dining and living room area. This increases the chance of catching a burglar who has defeated the window or door sensors. To be clever, I would put it in the same zone as the PIR sensor. That way, if the perimeter is bypassed, the door will still be alarmed.

You will notice that off the dining room is a patio door. You can probably protect this with a standard door sensor. Depending on how large the door is, you may have to use a sensor like the one for the garage door.

Our final challenge is the bay window in the living room. Some of these windows have small side windows that open. These should be protected with door/window sensors. If you have the funds, you might also want to install a glass break detector in case someone puts a brick through your front window. You can put the glass break sensor on either the window switch zone or PIR zone. It will probably come down to whatever is easiest from an installation perspective.

The second layer of protection is once again the passive infrared motion sensor.

What I would suggest is a PIR sensor in one corner of the living room and another in the kitchen. The kitchen one will guard the entrance from the mud room as well at the one from the garage and from the patio doors.

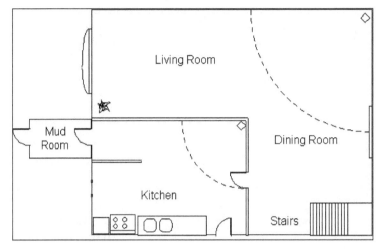

Living area PIRs

Now that we have finished protecting the ground floor, it is time to move upstairs. At this point you have a decision to make. You can continue with the layered-defense approach on the second floor and install alarm contacts on the windows, or not. I'll leave that decision up to the reader, because it may be a monetary one.

At the very least you should have PIR at the top of the stairs and one covering the main hallway. Depending on what you use your study for, you may want an alarm contact on the hallway door and a PIR sensor inside the study.

Anyone trying to break in through bedrooms 2 or 3 should be caught by either the PIR sensor at the top of the stairs or the one covering the main hall. The main hall PIR should be installed outside the master bedroom so that it looks down the hallway.

Before we move on to the installation step, I have a really simple alarm sensor you can make yourself that is just as good as the expensive ones you see in the department stores.

You have probably seen large items like BBQs, patio furniture, lawn mowers, and the like with a cable running through their handles so that they are all strung together. Here is how to make one of your very own for the price of some speaker wire and a resistor!

Simply solder a 5.6K ohm resistor across the two ends of the speaker wire. Now you have a loop with an end of line resistor that you can hook to your alarm system. (Or just twist the wires together if it isn't the end of line.)

Simply thread the speaker wire through whatever you want to protect. For example, the rear wheels of your bicycles or the handle of your BBQ. Put the resistor end in a tamper proof box of some sort and fasten it to something solid. Connect the other end of the wire to your zone. If you will be using the loop outdoors, I would suggest potting the resistor in epoxy or silicone rubber.

You now have the same system as a big box store, at a fraction of the price!

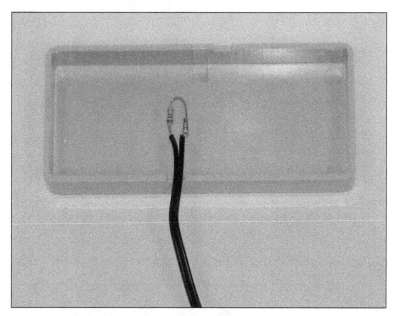

Wire loop sensor

Step 3 – the installation

In this step we will be doing the actual installation and wiring of the sensors. It is in this step that your carpentry skills will be put to test.

Switch contact wiring

This wiring method is for any non-powered switch, for example, door and window contacts, the garage door contacts, or the loop sensor. The sensor itself is not powered, so connecting them in series is simple.

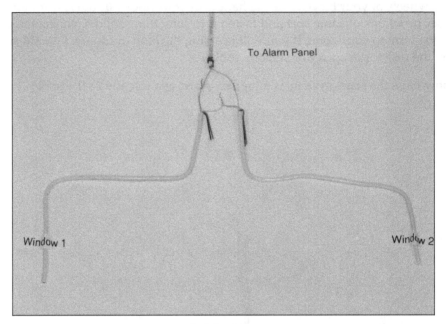

Switch wiring

The previous photograph and the following diagram show how this is done:

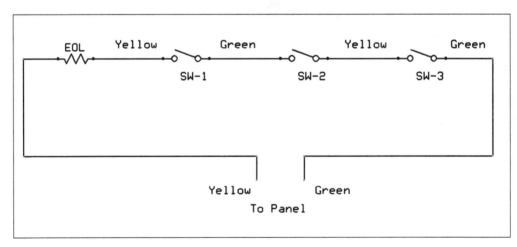

Switch wiring (schematic)

As you can see, you simply keep connecting the yellow wire of one set of contacts to the green of the next, until you have all of the contacts wired in series.

Window and door contact wiring

Sensors such as PIRs, glass break detectors, and smoke detectors require power. This makes them a bit more complex to install. If you are following my layered-defense technique, then there will never be a need to have active sensors (PIRs) and passive sensors (window contacts) in the same zone.

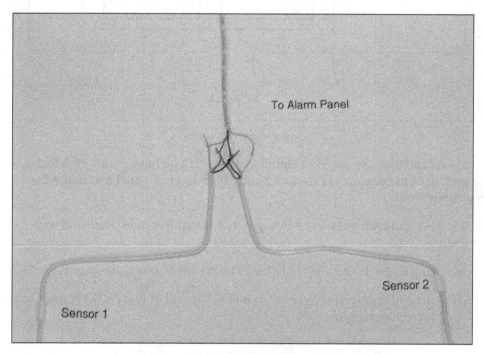

Active sensor wiring

The only difference between the two wiring examples is that the power is connected in *parallel* and the contacts are connected in *series*.

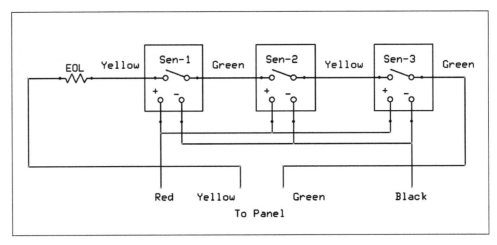

Sensor wiring (schematic)

These two examples use the least amount of wire. If you have plenty of wire, then pull all of the sensor and contact wiring back to your panel and make the connections there.

This is a more professional way of doing it, but it requires more wire and more wire fishing.

If I was wiring a new home with only bare studs visible, this is the way I would do it.

The following photographs show how to install the end of line (EOL) resistor in the window contact assembly.

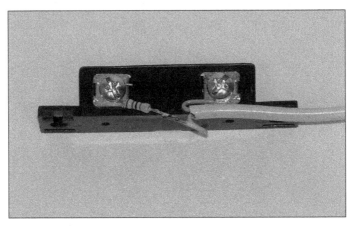

EOL resistor outside a door contact

Wrap one of the resistor leads around one of the screw terminals and solder it to the yellow conductor of the wire leading to the contacts. Wrap the green wire around the other terminal. Keep the wires as short as possible so that they can be tucked neatly into the case of the contacts.

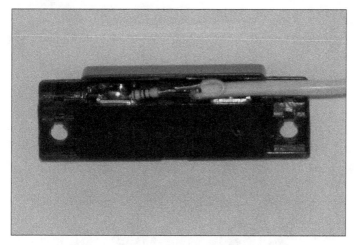

EOL resistor inside a door contact (bottom view)

Here, we see the end of line resistor neatly stowed into the case of the window contact.

Assembled window contact (top view)

The idea is that once the contacts are mounted onto the door or window frame, the contacts with the EOL resistor will look exactly like all of the other contacts and the burglar will have no idea which set of contacts contains the end of line resistor.

Active sensor wiring

The only difference between wiring a door or window contact sensor and an active sensor is that you must also connect power to it. You may have noticed that I have been using yellow and green for the contact wires. That is because we are now going to use red and black for power wiring.

The red wire is connected to the +12 volts at the panel and the black is the negative.

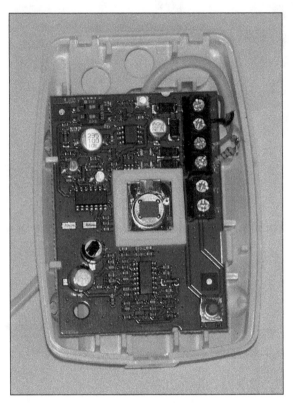

PIR with EOL installed inside

The preceding photograph shows the inside of a PIR sensor with an end of line resistor installed. Many sensors come with an *anti-tamper* switch built in. This is the small red button you see in the lower-right corner of the PCB. The contacts marked **TAMP** are connected in series with the alarm contacts. That way if anyone opens the case, the alarm will sound. So there is no need to hide the end of line resistor.

Any of the other types of sensors you are likely to install will be the same as the PIR sensor. The only difference is that CO and smoke detectors may not have anti-tamper switches.

The software

The software consists of two modules, which you will find in the Cloud9 directory. For those of you who don't know, you access the Cloud9 IDE by entering `<bone I/P address>:3000` in your web browser.

In my case it looks like, `192.168.10.105:3000`.

The two modules are called `Alarmpnl.js` and `Alarmpnl.html`. In order to run the software, simply select `Alarmpnl.js` from the menu and click on **Run**.

In the console at the bottom of the screen you will eventually see a message telling you the IP address of the web page that it loaded. Again in my case it is `192.168.10.105:8000`. This is because the software is using port 8000.

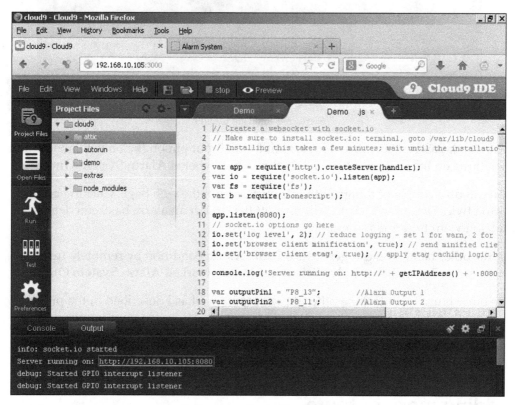

Software running in Cloud9 IDE

In the following screenshot, we see the result of copying the IP address from the **Cloud9 console** into the tab of a web browser. You can do this by simply double-clicking on the blue text. This will open the page in a new tab of your current window.

Note the address in the browser bar.

The software uses port 8080 of the BeagleBone IP address, which in my case is `192.168.10.105`.

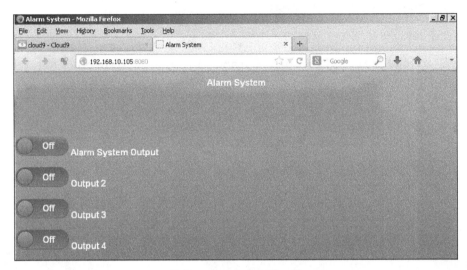

Software running in Cloud9

What the JavaScript software does is wait for an input pin on the bone to go low and then turns on the output one, which in this case is labeled **Alarm System Output**.

You can do a couple of things with this output from the web page. Clicking on the button twice (*not* double-click) will turn off the siren if an alarm has been detected and you want to cancel it remotely.

On the other hand, you can generate a **Panic Alarm** condition by remotely turning on the siren. To do this, simply click on the button marked **Alarm System Output**.

The other buttons control the other three outputs, and as I described in the previous chapter, they can be used to turn on and off various devices in your home or office.

I would suggest that you change the label for the button to reflect what it is actually connected to; for example **Front Gate** or **Emergency Pump**.

Adding more outputs

In order to add more outputs to our system, we must make some modifications to the two pieces of code provided with the book.

First we must modify the JavaScript as follows:

```
socket.on('Output4', function (data) {
    if (data == 'on') {
        //Turn the LED ON
        b.digitalWrite(outputPin4,1);
        console.log ("LED 4 On");
    } else if (data == 'off') {
        //Turn the LED OFF
        b.digitalWrite(outputPin4,0);
        console.log ("LED 4 Off");
    }
});
```

In the code snippet above, `outputPin4` is a variable corresponding to an actual pin on the BeagleBone.

These variables were assigned earlier in the code:

```
var outputPin1 = "P8_13";        //Alarm Output 1
var outputPin2 = 'P8_11';        //Alarm Output 2
var outputPin3 = 'P8_12';        //Alarm Output 3
var outputPin4 = 'P8_14';        //Alarm Output 4
```

In order to add another output, you would replicate this code and change the highlighted code from output4 to output5 for example, change `outputPin4` to `outputPin5`.

You would then have to add a variable called `outputPin5` and assign it to an actual I/O pin on the BeagleBone.

You must also modify the HTML page to add another switch icon to the page.

In this case you must change all references to `switch4`, `output4`, and `toggleswitch4` to `switch5`, `output5`, and `toggleswitch5` respectively.

```
<div data-role="fieldcontain">
<select name="toggleswitch4" id="Output4" data-theme="b"
  data-role="slider" onchange="Switch4(this);">
  <option value="off">
  Off
  </option>
  <option value="on">
    On
  </option>
```

```
</select>
<label for="toggleswitch4">
  Output 4
</label>
</div>
```

If you want to change the name of the switch as it appears on the web page, simply change the switch <label>. In this case Output 4 could be changed to Pump.

```
</select>
<label for="toggleswitch4">
  Output 4
</label>
</div>
```

The code is well documented and you can preview the page before actually running the software. In order to preview however, you have to save the file. So I would suggest giving it a different file name until you are sure it is the way you like it.

Adding more inputs

Adding inputs is much the same as adding outputs. We must modify the JavaScript file.

First we add a new input pin:

```
var inputPin1 = 'P8_19';     //Zone 1
var inputPin2 = 'P8_15';     //Zone 2
var inputPin3 = 'P8_9';      //Zone 3
var inputPin4 = 'P8_7';      //Zone 4
var inputPin5 = 'p8_ ?';           //Zone 5

//Setup pin directions
b.pinMode(inputPin1, b.INPUT);
b.pinMode(inputPin2, b.INPUT);
b.pinMode(inputPin3, b.INPUT);
b.pinMode(inputPin4, b.INPUT);
b.pinMode(inputPin5, b.INPUT);
```

The next thing we do is add another interrupt handler:

```
// Setup interupts
b.attachInterrupt(inputPin1, true, b.FALLING, Zone1Callback);
b.attachInterrupt(inputPin2, true, b.FALLING, Zone2Callback);
b.attachInterrupt(inputPin3, true, b.FALLING, Zone3Callback);
b.attachInterrupt(inputPin4, true, b.FALLING, Zone4Callback);
b.attachInterrupt(inputPin5, true, b.FALLING, Zone5Callback);
```

Now, all we have to do is tell BeagleBone to turn on the alarm siren when the interrupt occurs:

```
//Alarm Detected in Zone 5
function Zone5Callback() {
  flag4 ++;
  if (flag4 > 1){   //For false alarms on script startup
    console.log ("Alarm Detected in Zone 5");
    Alarm();
    state = 1;
    b.digitalWrite(outputPin1, state);//Turn ON the Alarm LED
  }
}
```

The software uses a JavaScript package called jQuery and another called jQuery mobile, these two packages allow us to use the web page with mobile devices. An approximation of the software running on a mobile device is shown in the following screenshot:

Web page on a mobile device

The following screenshot shows the web page as it might be displayed on a tablet or a laptop:

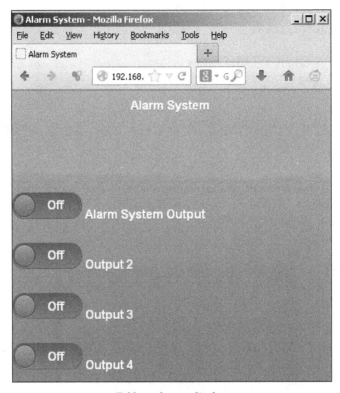

Tablet or laptop display

 On a laptop, the page will automatically expand to fit the browser window.

The table below shows the common I/O pins to both the boards

P9			P8		
GPIO	Pin #	Signal	GPIO	Pin #	Signal
30	11	Not Used	66	7 *	Zone 4 Input
60	12	Not Used	67	8	Not Used
31	13	Not Used	69	9 *	Zone 3 Input
40	14	Not Used	68	10	Not Used
48	15	Not Used	45	11 *	Alarm Output 2
			44	12	Not Used

P9			P8		
4	17 *	Alarm Output 3	23	13 *	Alarm Output 1
			26	14	Not Used
I2C2	19	Used by Beagle	47	15 *	Zone 2 Input
			46	16	Not Used
3	21 *	Alarm Output 4	27	17 *	Key Switch Input
			65	18	Not Used
49	23	Not Used	22	19 *	Zone 1 Input

BeagleBone I/O pins

The operating system image that comes with this book is supposed to work on either the **BeagleBone White** or the newer **BeagleBone Black**. The black uses some of the I/O for the LCD display and the **eMMC** chip; so in order to make the alarm system hardware work with either version, we must take care not to use any of the I/O used by the black.

The pins marked with an * are the ones currently used by the software in this book.

Pins that are marked as *Not Used* should be safe for you to use for future expansion, subject to changes in the Kernel (if you upgrade).

Summary

In this chapter we learned how to plan our alarm system, from the first walkabout to the final installation.

We also learned how to run and modify the software to suit our needs.

We learned how to add more zone inputs and more outputs to the software.

In the next two chapters we will build and test the hardware, which we will be installing in our dream home.

When it comes to installation, there is an excellent website that will help you considerably. This site tells you how to install many different types of low voltage household wiring. You can find it at http://www.structuredhomewiring.com/AlarmWiring.aspx.

4

Building the Hardware

In this chapter we will build the actual alarm system hardware. I have chosen a modular design for the hardware. The hardware consists of three different PCBs or modules; they are as follows.

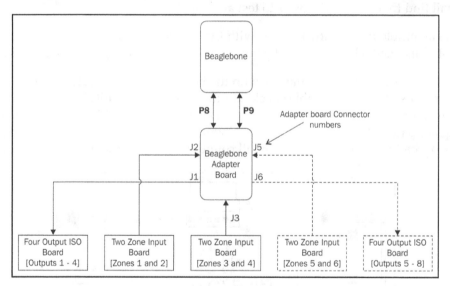

- The first is the module that monitors various zones. In this case, two zones; so, we will be building two identical PCBs in order to monitor four zones. If you want to add zones, just build more zone modules and modify the software (the procedure for doing this was described in *Chapter 3*, *Bigger and Better*).The additional modules are shown by dashed lines in the preceding diagram.

- The second module is the optically isolated output board. This is the board that is used to activate lights, sirens, and so on. You can control up to four devices with this board.

- The third board is the one that makes this project a BeagleBone project. What this does is connect the other boards to BeagleBone. If you want to add zones or outputs, this is the part of the hardware that you would modify.

This book uses the original BeagleBone board as the alarm system controller. However, any microcomputer board with input-output capability can be used with this hardware. For example, the RaspberryPi or the Arduino-based systems. For that matter, it is probably possible to use BeagleBoard as well.

Hopefully, this book provides sufficient documentation for an advanced user to adapt the hardware to his or her board.

Zone monitor PCB

This is a relatively simple board to assemble. All of the parts used in this project are thru-hole parts; so, no advanced surface mount soldering skills are required. Also, you will find that it is much easier to test and repair.

When I assemble PCBs, I always start with the lowest parts and work towards the highest. This way, when you flip the board on its back, all the parts don't fall out!

Just follow the parts list and silkscreen on the board, and you should not have any problems. Just be sure to double check that the integrated circuits **U1** and **U2** are installed correctly. The LEDs and diodes are also polarity sensitive. On both devices, the square pad on the PCB is pin 1. The IC will have either a notch milled into it as, shown in the following figure, or a small round indentation that indicates pin 1.

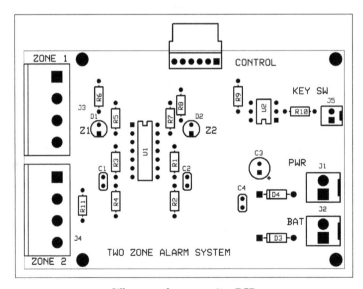

Silkscreen of zone monitor PCB

Connectors **J3** and **J4** on the zone monitor schematic are your connections to the zones that you wish to monitor. Pins 1 and 2 of each connector are the zone inputs. Pins 3 and 4 are used to supply power to the PIRs and other active sensors. Pin 4, which is called **GND** or ground, is the +12V return. It is not the same as the **COM** or common input.

Connector **J5** is the key switch input. Applying +12V to pin 2 and grounding pin 1 will turn on the opto-isolator U2. This will pull the **/key** signal low.

This +12V can come from a key switch, a push button switch, a toggle switch, or anything you like as long as it applies +12V to the opto-isolator.

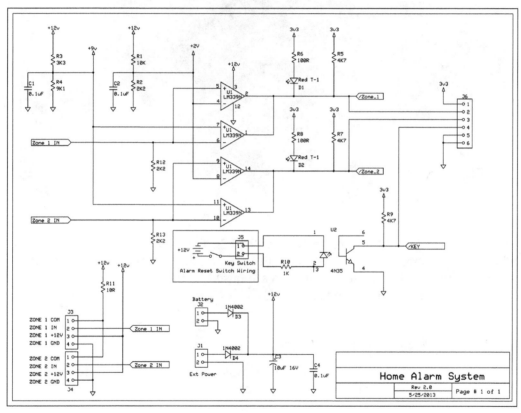

Zone monitor schematic

The following photograph shows the completed PCB.

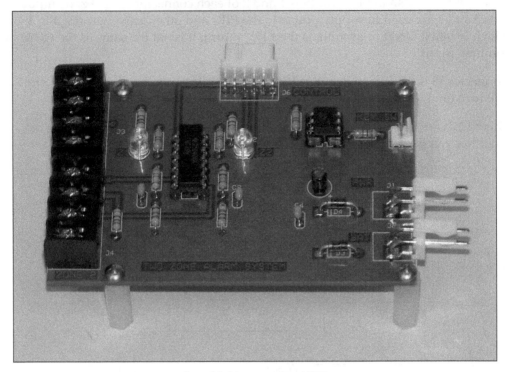

Assembled two zone input PCB

You will notice that I have used sockets for the ICs. This is not strictly necessary, but when I build prototypes, I use sockets until I am sure that the design will work. Also notice that the rectifier diodes **D3** and **D4** are raised off the board. This is to allow better cooling, should they need it.

Isolated output PCB

The optically isolated output PCB is a very simple construction. There are two reasons why I made a separate board in this case.

This form factor allows for a more modular design. You can have as many outputs as you can find I/O pins on BeagleBone.

It is also cheaper to order small 3.8" x 2.5" mini boards from **ExpressPCB** than to order a larger custom-size board.

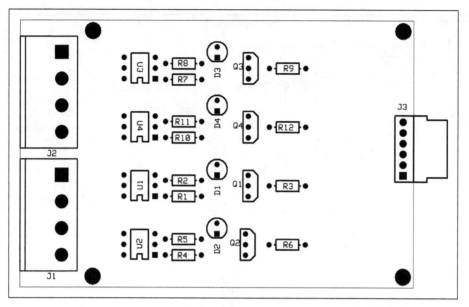

Isolated output PCB

Assembly of this board is very much the same as that of the first board.

1. Install the resistors first.
2. Install the LEDs, making sure that the polarity is correct.
3. Install the transistors, again checking for correct installation.

4. Install the ICs preferably on sockets to make repairs easier.

5. Finally, install the connectors.

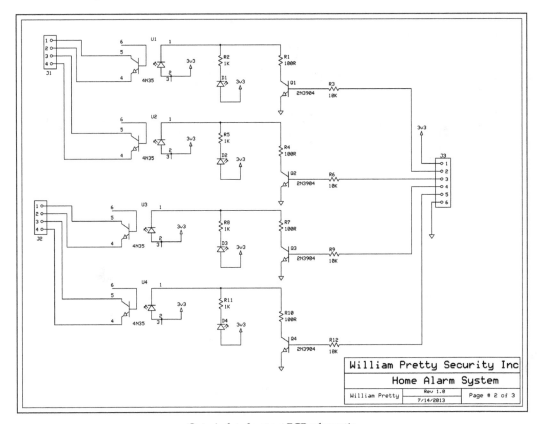

Opto-isolated output PCB schematic

All four circuits are identical. A logical 1 on the input applies 3.3V to the base of the NPN transistor. This turns on the transistor and pulls the collector of the transistor low. This turns on the status LED [**D1** – **D4**] and the LED portion of the **4N35** opto-isolator. When the internal LED is turned on, it turns on the internal transistor. The status LED is provided for debugging purposes. The status LED turns on when the opto-isolator is activated.

Assembled opto-isolator output PCB

The preceding photograph shows the assembled PCB. Observant readers may notice that the color code of the 1K resistor for the first output is different from the rest. This resistor is what you are probably used to and has the normal 5 percent color code.

Brown, black, red, and gold means (1 - 0) x 100 with a 5 percent tolerance, that is, 1000 ohms.

The other resistors are 1 percent tolerance resistors; so, three decimal places are required.

So, brown, black, black, and brown means, (1 - 0 - 0) x 10 with a 1 percent tolerance, that is, 1000 ohms.

There is no need to use 1 percent resistors in this design. I had them in my lab stock; so, I used them.

You will also note that the white connector hangs over the edge of the board. This is to make it easier to attach the connector when the boards are stacked during the final assembly.

Connecting devices to the board

Congratulations! You now have a finished PCB capable of turning 3.3V logic signals into a real world action. Not only can you turn on lights and sirens, you can also use this board to turn on your lawn sprinkler!

The following are two methods of doing just that.

The diagram below shows a small relay connected directly to the output transistor of the opto-isolator. If you want to maintain isolation between the alarm panel and the device you are controlling, the +12V that is powering the relay should have a separate ground return from the panel ground.

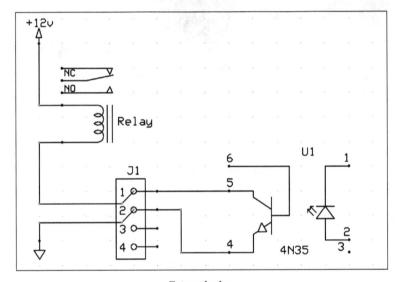

External relay

You can now hook your siren or flashing light to the contacts of the mechanical relay without any fear of blowing the output transistor of the onboard isolator. Accidents happen, and that is why I suggested putting the 4N35s on sockets. They aren't that expensive; so, I suggest you order spares.

In this case, we are using one opto-isolator to drive another opto-isolator. In schematic form, this probably looks a bit odd. However, in the real world, the second isolator can be a high-current device that is capable of switching high voltage and current. In addition to the transistor shown in the drawing, it is also possible to buy opto-isolators with triac outputs for switching AC loads.

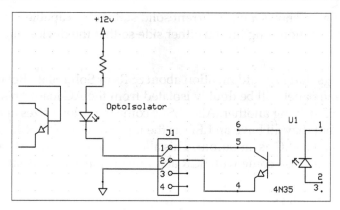

External opto-isolator

An example of one such AC load might be the motor that opens and closes your garage door or the gate at the end of your lane way.

[Wiring of such high voltage and high current loads should probably be left to your local licensed electrician. Meeting the local electrical codes is up to you. Because the system was built by you, it will NOT be CSA/UL approved, and the electrician may not want to install or connect it.]

Another application of this type of relay would be to turn on exterior lighting. This could be done either automatically using a zone input and a light sensor or remotely by connecting to the panel via the Internet.

More on remote control later.

Typical Solid State Relay

The preceding figure shows a high current solid state relay capable of switching AC loads. Note the two mounting fins on either side so that the device can be mounted on a heat sink.

A couple of things that I should mention about SSRs or Solid State Relays is that in this project, the panel will be doubly isolated from the AC load. This is because you have one SSR driving another. Also, SSRs come in various sizes and output configurations, but they all have an LED as the input device. The SSR in the photograph has a **TRIAC** as an output. This allows you to control AC devices like motors. These relays also come with SCR and power transistor outputs.

Helpful links

TRIAC: `http://en.wikipedia.org/wiki/TRIAC`

SCR: `http://en.wikipedia.org/wiki/Silicon-controlled_rectifier`

You will remember that in *Chapter 1, Alarm Systems 101,* I said that all alarm systems monitor contacts and perform some actions based on the changes that they see.

One handy use of an AC relay might be to turn on a backup sump pump if the alarm system detects a flood and the primary pump has failed. This would be handy for those of us who live in low-lying areas.

BeagleBone adapter PCB

This is where our project comes together and becomes an actual BeagleBone-controlled alarm system. What this board does is connect BeagleBone to the other boards. I have provided you with a third PCB that brings out the I/O pins that the software will use. If you wish, you can build your own using a **ProtoBoard** such as the one from **Circuitco**.

The table below shows some of the GPIO pins that are set by default to the GPIO mode without the use of overlays or mux tables.

The pins marked with an * are the ones currently used by the software in this book.

The pins marked with a ~ have been routed for future expansion.

P9				P8			
GPIO	Pin #	GPIO	Pin	GPIO	Pin #	GPIO	Pin
30	11	60	12 ~	66	7 *	67	8
31	13	40	14 ~	69	9 *	68	10
48	15	51	16 ~	45	11 *	44	12
4	17 *	5	18 ~	23	13 *	26	14
	19			47	15 *	46	16
3	21 *	2	22 ~	27	17 *	65	18
49	23	15	24 ~	22	19 *		
117	25	14	26 ~				
125	27						

Link

Circuitco: http://circuitco.com/support/index.
php?title=BeagleBone_Breadboard

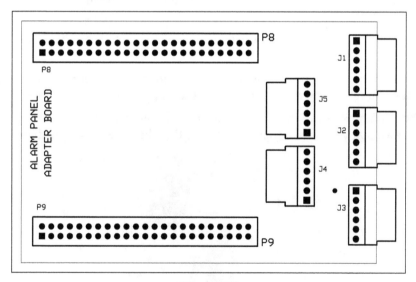

Adapter PCB

The connectors on the Adapter PCB have the following uses in the software that accompanies this book:

1. Connector **J2** is for "Zones 1 and 2" inputs, connector **J3** is for "Zone 3 and 4" inputs, and connector **J1** is for "Outputs 1 to 4".

2. Pins 12, 14, and 16 have been routed to connector **J5**, which is labelled as "Zones 5 and 6" on the schematic.

3. Pins 18, 22, 24, and 26 have been routed to connector **J4**, which is labelled as "Outputs 5 to 8" on the schematic.

4. You should be aware that these pins can be programmed to be either inputs or outputs. What you use them for is up to you. The BeagleBone +3.3V supply and ground is also connected to these headers, should you require them.

Mechanical PCB assembly

There are two types of 5/8" long nylon spacers in the parts list. One type has a 4-40 screw attached to it. The other type does not.

1. Starting with the PCB at the bottom, use the spacers with the 4-40 screw attached to them and fasten this PCB to the PC in the middle, using four more of the same type of spacer.

2. You should now have two boards fastened together with the four exposed 4-40 nylon screws.

3. Install the other type of 5/8" spacer (without the 4-40 screws attached) on these screws using the spacer as a nut to hold the boards together.

4. You can now install the PCB at the top to theses spacers using any type of 4-40 screws that you have at hand, provided that they are no longer than 3/8".

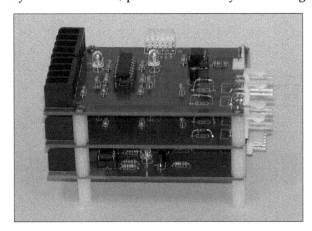

Assembled alarm system PCBs

If you have made it this far and your assembly looks like the preceding photograph, congratulations! You have just finished assembling the PCBs for your alarm system.

You can stack the PCBs in any order you like. I chose to put the zone boards on top and the output board at the bottom.

Wiring harness assembly

You will need three harnesses like the one shown in the following figure. I used a red wire to indicate pin 1. This is not strictly necessary because the connectors are keyed.

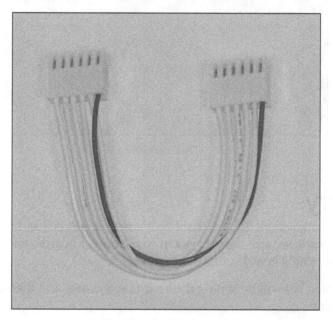

Zone board wiring harness

As far as the wire goes, any 24AWG wire will fit the connector pins. You can even use wires salvaged from an old PC power supply if you like.

The harness is basically a one-to-one connection between the two connectors. While Digikey and others probably sell a hand tool for crimping the connector pins, I found the price too high to justify for just one project. I just used a pair of needle nose pliers to hand crimp the pins. It takes longer and requires a bit of practice, but the price is right and there aren't that many pins to crimp.

Test harness

The purpose of this harness is to connect the zone and output boards to BeagleBone without the use of the BeagleBone adapter board. What I did was crimp jumper wires into a connector so that I can easily and safely connect the board that I am testing to BeagleBone or the outside world in general.

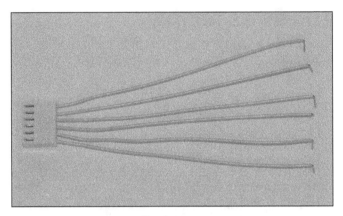

Test harness

Summary

In this chapter, we assembled the actual hardware that will be used in the alarm system. At this point, we still have a system consisting of boards, which can be connected to any single board computer system.

In the next chapter, we will be testing the boards separately and then connecting them to BeagleBone.

5
Testing the Hardware

In the previous chapter we built the hardware for our alarm system. Now it is time to test the hardware. We will do that by first testing it without the BeagleBone attached. The boards that we built have built-in test LEDs, which will allow us to test the hardware without running any software, or even connecting the hardware to a computer.

You will find this feature handy when you actually install the sensors. You can have a partner-walk-around trip sensors, and open and close windows and doors, all without running any software. Basically, if the zone LED goes on and off when you open and close an alarm circuit, your wiring is good.

The test equipment

In order to test the alarm system board, you will need the following two pieces of lab equipment:

1. A variable dual power supply capable of supplying up to 15V and about 2 amps. The supply should also have current limiting.

2. A multimeter capable of measuring up to about 15V DC supply with a milliamp scale as well.

Both of these are readily available on eBay and elsewhere. My local hardware store regularly sells multimeters for about $20.

If you don't have or can't afford a variable power supply, use AAA batteries in series to get yourself a 13.5V and a 3V supply. The batteries won't supply enough current to do any serious damage, in case of the 13.5V version.

A 13.5V DC supply consists of nine 1.5V batteries connected together in series.

A 3V DC supply is two AAA batteries connected in series. This will be used to simulate the 3.3V supply from the BeagleBone.

Visual check

Before we actually power up the board for the first time, we need to do the following basic visual checks:

1. Check if the diodes and transistors are installed properly.
2. The band on the rectifier diodes should match the outline on the silkscreen.
3. The case of the transistors and LEDs should match the pattern on the silkscreen.
4. Check if pin 1 on the IC is in the correct position. (The IC hasn't been placed backwards!)

If all of these are checked, then you are ready to apply power to the board.

If everything appears to be correct, then you are ready to proceed to the next step.

The zone input board

The following series of steps will test the zone board, which the alarm system will use to talk to detect changes in the outside world.

Power check

Now that we have completed our visual check of the board and fixed the errors, it is time to apply power to the board.

1. Apply 13.5V DC supply to either **J1** or **J2** of the board.
2. Connect the negative lead of the multimeter to pin 2 of either J1 or J2.
3. Measure the voltage at the anode (end without the stripe) of **D4** or **D5**, depending on which connector you chose.
4. Make a note of this voltage.
5. Measure the voltage at the cathode (stripe) end of the diode. The voltage should be about 0.7V less than the voltage on the anode. (This is because there is about a 0.7V across the PN junction of most rectifier diodes.)

6. Apply 3.3V (or 3V if you are using batteries) to pins 1 and 6 of **J6**. Be CAREFUL because there is no polarity protection on this connector. Pin 1 is the positive terminal and pin 6 is the negative or the ground terminal.

7. You should measure 3.3V between pin 1 and the ground terminal with the meter.

8. If these measurements are correct, you can remove the power for now.

Troubleshooting power problems

The most common problem you will find here is a reversed diode. Remember that the position of the stripe on the diode must match the stripe on the silkscreen.

Other than that, check for poor solder joints.

Zone input tests

Now that we have completed the power test, it is time to see if the board actually works.

In the following steps, we are simulating a zone that has been connected to the alarm system:

1. Connect a 5.6K ohm resistor in series with an SPDT (single pole double throw) switch, and connect this between the COM terminal (1) and the ZONE terminal (2) on the terminal strip. See the following figure; make sure the switch is closed so that the 5.6K ohm resistor is connected across pins 1 and 2.

Zone input EOL resistor

2. Apply both 13.5V and 3.3V power to the board.

3. The LED associated with the zone you are testing should be off.

4. Change the switch position so that the connection is now open. This simulates an alarm condition.

5. The LED associated with the zone you are testing should turn on.

6. Do this test for both the zones.

Alarm output board tests

The following series of steps will test the output board, which the alarm system will use to talk to the outside world.

The following figure shows the test fixture that I built using a common protoboard.

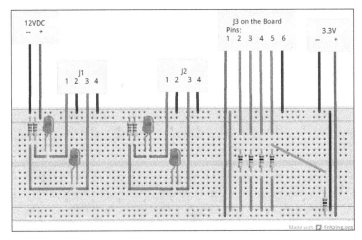

Protoboard test fixture

From left to right, the output of the opto-isolator is connected to an LED. The emitter of the opto-isolator is connected to the ground terminal, while the collector is connected to the cathode of an LED. This LED is in turn connected to +12V through a 2.2K ohm resistor. When the opto-isolator is turned on, current flows from the collector to the emitter and the LED turns on. There are two identical circuits here; one for each output connector.

Connector **J3** from the board is connected to 3.3V and four pull-down resistors. There is a 1K ohm resistor that is used to simulate the output of the BeagleBone. By connecting the orange wire to the various inputs, you can simulate a logical 1 on the input and turn on the opto-isolator. You will recall that we built a six-pin test connector in the previous chapter. It is this connector that you should use to connect the board you are testing to the protoboard. You can use any kind of 24AWG solid wire to connect J1 and J2 to the protoboard. *SparkFun* sells jumper packs for just this purpose.

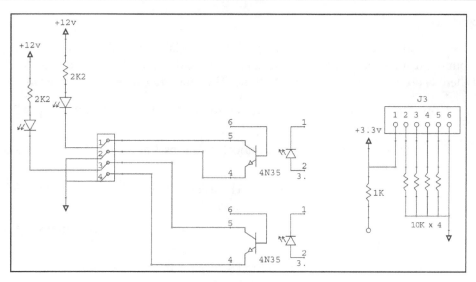

Protoboard schematic

For those of you who prefer schematics, the previous figure shows a schematic representation of the test fixture.

The 10K resistors are pull-downs that hold the input at logic 0. When you connect the 1K resistor to one of the pins of J3, you are applying logic 1 to the input. This simulates the output of the BeagleBone.

Output board

Testing

What we are about to do in the following tests is simulate the BeagleBone outputs without using an actual BeagleBone. In that way, we don't need any special software and there is no risk to our actual BeagleBone. The following steps show how we do it:

1. Connect the orange wire from the 1K resistor to the wire leading to pin 2 of J3.

2. D1 should light, and the LED connected to pins 1 and 2 of terminal strip J1 should light.

3. Connect the orange wire from the 1K resistor to the wire leading to pin 3 of J3.

4. D2 should light, and the LED connected to pins 3 and 4 of terminal strip J1 should light.

5. Connect the orange wire from the 1K resistor to the wire leading to pin 4 of J3.

6. D3 should light, and the LED connected to pins 1 and 2 of terminal strip J2 should light.

7. Connect the orange wire from the 1K resistor to the wire leading to pin 5 of J3.

8. D4 should light, and the LED connected to pins 3 and 4 of terminal strip J2 should light.

Summary

In this chapter we tested the hardware that we built in the previous chapters. If you like, you can use the zone-testing portion of this chapter to test your actual installation wiring. Remember that you do not need the BeagleBone to test your wiring. That's what the LEDs are for.

In the next chapter we will learn how to use any unused outputs on the alarm system to control other things such as pumps and sprinklers.

6
Automating Stuff

In the previous chapters we built and tested hardware for our alarm system. If you recall, the basic system came with four optically isolated outputs. If we assume that one output will be used to activate the strobe light and/or a siren (you can hook the two in parallel so long as they are both the same voltage, using a relay as shown at the end of *Chapter 4*, *Building the Hardware*), we are then left with three unused outputs. The BeagleBone adapter board also gives us the hardware capability to drive even more outputs. So now I am going to give some ideas about things you can do with these leftover outputs.

The low-current solenoid driver

The low-current solenoid driver circuit can be used to control things such as the small solenoids used by many lawn sprinkler systems.

The data sheet says that the IC is capable of providing 2A continuously, provided that it has a proper heat sink. Fortunately, we will only be pulsing the solenoid on for about a second, so this should not be a problem.

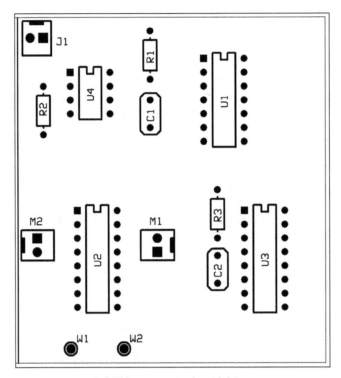

A dual low-current solenoid driver

Our circuit will drive two solenoids at the same time; for example, two sprinklers. We cannot control solenoids separately because we need to keep the design simple and maintain the number of inputs required. Therefore, you will have to turn on both sprinklers at once.

The following circuit is used to drive a single-coil solenoid. This type of solenoid requires a dual polarity pulse to activate it. A positive-going pulse opens the solenoid and a negative-going pulse closes it. In order to do this, we will use what is called a **half-bridge circuit**. The **SN754410** IC is designed to control a full-bridge circuit, so we get two solenoid controllers for the price of one!

The **LM555 timer (U4)** generates a one-second pulse when it receives a trigger pulse from the alarm board. I used the **LM555** timer to save us the trouble of having to generate the trigger pulse in software.

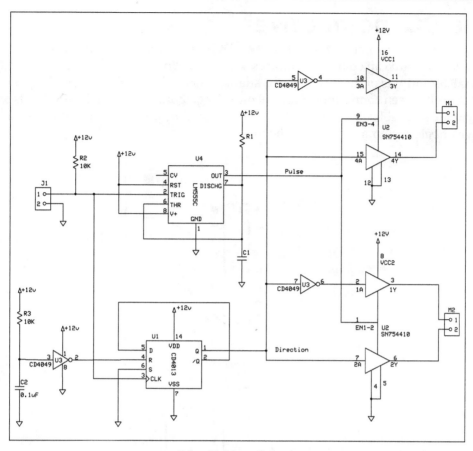

Solenoid driver schematic

As I said before, you have to change the polarity of the pulse to open and close the valve and that is what the **CD4013** flip-flop is for. The polarity of the pulse changes every time the circuit is triggered. To generate the pulse, we simply enable the **SN754410** IC with a one-second pulse. The solenoids are connected to the **M1** or **M2** connector.

The DC-motor driver

The DC-motor driver circuit will drive two DC motors, and unlike the solenoid driver, this board can control the motors separately. You can also connect it directly to the 3.3V outputs of the BeagleBoard adapter board. The PCB has been designed so that it fits between connectors **J8** and **J9** on a BeagleBone prototype board. Expansion boards are stackable on the BeagleBone, so it should be possible to put this board above or below your alarm system boards.

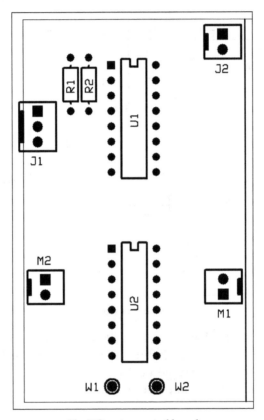

The DC motor control board

In this case, the motor will be powered continuously as compared to the solenoid, which is pulsed. For this reason, it will be a good idea to install a heat sink on **U2**.

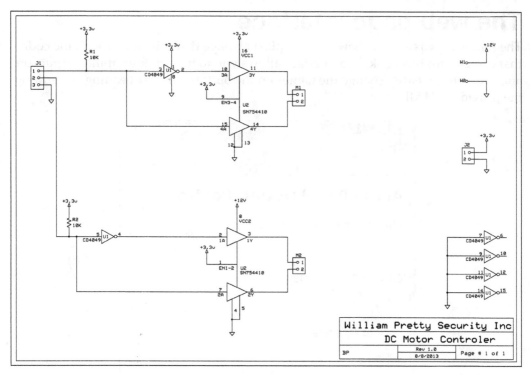

In the preceding diagram, you will notice that the motor driver **IC**, **U2**, has two VCC inputs. The VCC input is the power supply input to an IC, which normally has only one supply input. The great thing about **SN754410** is that it has two supply inputs. One for the control logic, in this case 3.3V, and one for the output driver circuit (12V). In this way, we can control a 12-volt device with 3.3-volt logic.

What the DC motor does is up to you; for example, a 12-volt bilge pump, a fountain pump in your garden, or perhaps some low-voltage LED lighting.

The web page interface

The following screenshot shows the simple web page that is included with the code that comes with this book. The interface allows you to turn all four of the outputs on and off. You can easily change the names on the buttons and the headings by editing the provided HTML code.

The web interface

The web page is hosted by the BeagleBone/Alarm system, using the BeagleBone's built-in socket server.

What this means is that you can use your smart phone to access the alarm remotely so as to:

- Turn low-voltage lighting on and off by driving a relay from one of the outputs
- Turn your sprinkler system on or off using an output and the solenoid board
- Open or close your electric blinds using the DC motor controller board
- Open your garage door by connecting a relay across the manual open button that comes with the door
- You can even use your smart phone as a panic button to activate the siren and strobe, if you can't reach the one you didn't think you would need!

Summary

In this chapter we introduced some additional uses of the alarm system hardware that are not found in budget or domestic alarm systems. By using the leftover outputs from the alarm system, we were able to remotely control things in the real world, such as sprinklers and outdoor lighting.

In the next chapter, we will be moving even further away from the conventional alarm system by using BeagleBone to monitor the status of our home network.

Don't forget we are connected to our home network, and the BeagleBone has a USB connector, which is just bound to come in handy!

7
Protecting Your Network

This chapter isn't so much about the physical alarm system per se as it is about protecting your home network from intruders. **BeagleBone** is connected to your home network, so it might as well do something in its spare time.

What we are going to do is install two small but very useful open source network monitoring software packages. The first package that we will be installing is MTR, which stands for **MyTraceRoute**. Anyone who has ever used trace route in either Linux or Windows will know that it is used to find the path to a given IP address.

MyTraceRoute

Installation could not be simpler. Perform the following steps for installing MyTraceRoute:

1. Change to the `/usr/src/` directory and then type:

   ```
   wget https://launchpad.net/mtr/main/0.85/+download/mtr-0.85.tar.gz
   ```

   This will download the gzip tar ball to the user source directory.

2. Then, unzip the file into the directory using the following command:

   ```
   tar -zxvf mtr-0.85.tar.gz.
   ```

3. Change to the directory that was created when the files were unzipped in the preceding step and type the following commands:

   ```
   ./configure
   make
   make install
   ```

   That's it. You are done.

File locations can be a moving target so if the preceding wget command doesn't work, a Google search should provide another location. The command is the same, but with a different web address.

Trace route examples

Here, we have a couple of examples of the software at work. This example shows the route from my lab computer to the Yahoo! site:

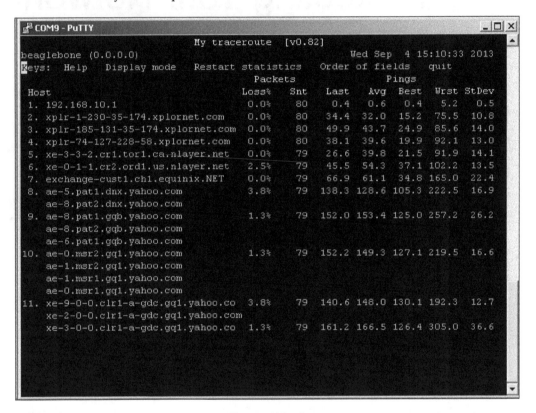

Route to Yahoo!

In this example, 192.168.10.1 is the Internet gateway on my system's router. Lines **2** to **4** are my Internet service provider XPLORNET. As you can see in the columns, the software not only provides the hops, but it also provides the time for each hop and the packet loss.

This example is the route to Packt Publishing or `www.packtpub.com`.

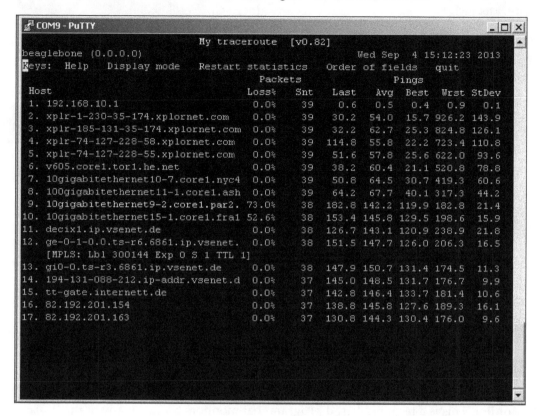

Route to www.packtpub.com

The path through my router and XPLORNET is much the same. However, note the packet loss at hosts 9 and 10.

Host 9 is showing a 73.0% packet loss! Host 10 isn't much better. If this were occurring on a host that you had access to, it might be worth looking into. At least if you are having download problems, you now know where to look for the source. For example, the bottleneck can sometimes be with you service provider. So, we have a handy tool that you can access remotely via SSH, as I described earlier in the book. Is that cool or what?

The following is an excerpt from the MTR documentation, which is installed when you make MTR:

SYNOPSIS

mtr [-hvrctglspeniu46] [--help] [--version] [--report]

[--report-wide]

[--report-cycles COUNT] [--curses] [--split] [--raw]

[--mpls] [--no-dns][--gtk][--address IP.ADD.RE.SS]

[--interval SECONDS][--psize BYTES | -s BYTES] HOSTNAME [PACKETSIZE]

More information on the use of MTR is installed when you enter make install. Simply enter man mtr (without the quotes) at the console.

IPTraf

The other package we will be installing is called **IPTraf**, which is short for **IP Traffic Monitor**. This is a terminal-based program that monitors traffic on any of the interfaces connected to your network or the BeagleBone.

Once again, we save the tar ball to the /usr/src directory and then unzip it to a directory:

1. First we get the tarball from the source website:

    ```
    wget https://fedorahosted.org/releases/i/p/iptraf-ng/
    iptraf-ng-1.1.4.tar.gz
    ```

2. Then, we untar it into a directory:

    ```
    tar -xzfv iptraf-ng-1.1.4.tar.gz
    ```

3. We then change to the iptraf-ng-1.1.4 directory, which was created previously.

4. Type the following commands to compile the source code:

```
./configure
make
make install
```

That's it we're done!

 One final note; file locations can be a moving target so if the preceding wget command doesn't work, a Google search should provide another location. The command is the same, but with a different web address.

Configuring IPTraf

Perform the following steps for configuring IPTraf:

1. We run the program by typing iptraf-ng in the terminal window. The following is the start screen:

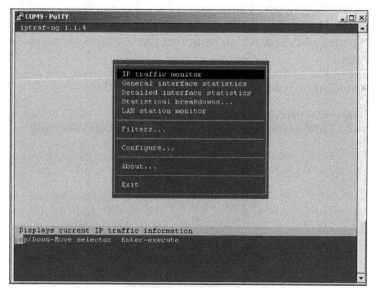

iptraf-ng start screen

2. The first thing we have to do is to configure the program options:

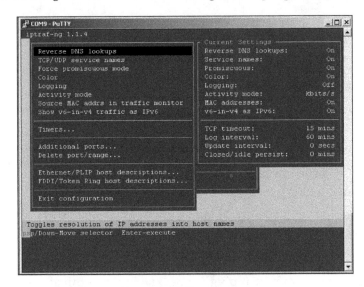

iptraf-ng configure screen

In the preceding figure, I have enabled all of the options, with the exception of logging. The up and down arrows on your terminal cause the menu bar to move up and down. A description of the feature appears in the box at the bottom.

3. The next thing we can do is set up some simple filters:

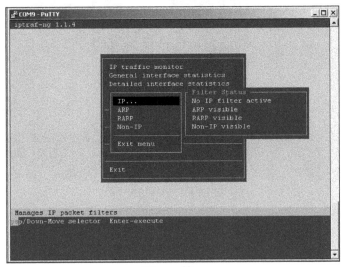

Set up a filter

4. The next step is to edit a filter. From the IP section, we select **Define New Filter**.

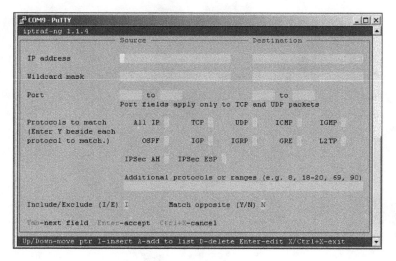

Define New Filter

5. We are now ready to enter some parameters. In my case, all I did was ask the software to track packets from a source address of `192.168.10.104`, which is one of the computers on my network.

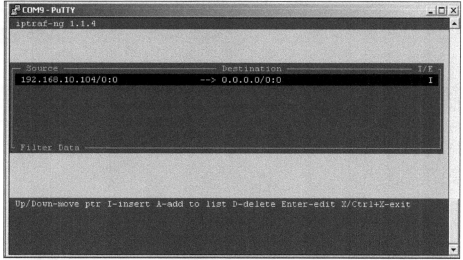

Filter data

6. Now that we have our software configured, it is time to run and see what we can find.

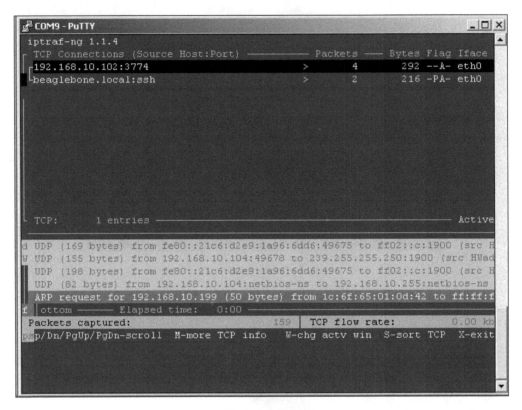

Capturing data

In the top portion of the window, we see the connections to etho on the BeagleBone. The first IP address is my lab computer, which I use for developing code. The second IP is a local connection that I made to BeagleBone via SSH. You will also notice an ARP request from one of my other PCs at the address 192.168.10.199.

Most of the other traffic is at the UDP packets 192.168.104, which (if you will recall) was the IP address in the filter we set up earlier.

For the skeptics in the audience, the following figure is the LAN computer's page of my wireless router.

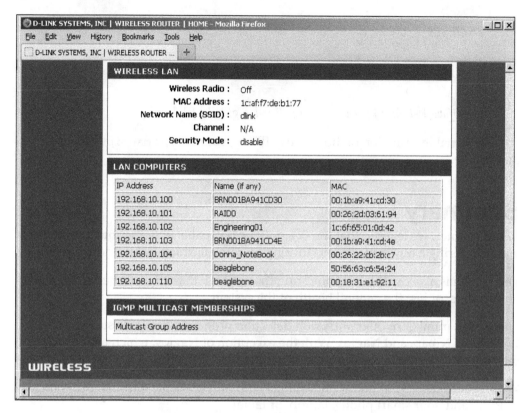

Network addresses

If you recall, I said that address `192.168.10.102` was my engineering lab computer. Also, my wife's notebook is the one we were filtering for, at `192.168.10.104`.

The BeagleBone appears twice on the list because one address is assigned to `eth0`, which is the actual Ethernet port (`192.168.10.105`), and another is probably the USB/LAN port (`192.168.10.110`).

You can also see my two network RAID drives at the addresses `192.168.10.100` and `192.168.10.101`.

The following is an excerpt from the IPTraf documentation, which is installed when you install IPTraf:

SYNOPSIS

iptraf { [-f] [-q] [-u] [{ -i iface | -g | -d iface | -s iface |

-z iface | -l iface } [-t timeout] [-B [-L logfile]]] | [-h] }

For additional information on how to use IPTraf, simply type `man iptraf` at the console.

Summary

In this chapter, we learned that the BeagleBone is capable of doing much more than just monitoring a few contacts and turning on some flashing lights and what not.

The system is also capable of monitoring the network that it is attached to for signs of intruders, or just the general health of the system.

There are a number of other intrusion detection programs available such as Wireshark, Nmap, and Nagios. With the exception of Nagios, which uses a web interface, all the others require a computer monitor, mouse, and keyboard to operate.

With your system, you can monitor things with only a simple terminal program such as Putty and your smart phone, laptop, or tablet.

In the next chapter, we will see how you can keep an eye on things while away from home.

So read on...

8
Keeping an Eye on Things

In this chapter, we will use a software package called Yaler to monitor our home network and alarm system from anywhere in the world where we can get an IP address. That's right; you can be at a café on the sidewalk in Paris and turn on the lawn sprinklers back in Houston.

 All of the following software comes preinstalled on the downloadable image. All you need to do is edit the appropriate files to add your own domain name. The rest is for those who want to "do it themselves" on another system.

Yaler

Yaler is an Internet relay site, which allows you to access your BeagleBone from any device with a web browser or an SSH client, or both. The Yaler project was set up specifically to serve the users of BeagleBone and Raspberry Pi. Yaler allows you to access your BeagleBone even though it is shielded by your home or office firewall.

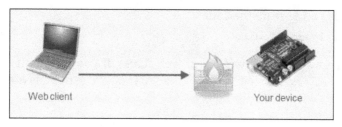

Normal access

Under normal circumstances, your firewall or mobile router blocks the access to your alarm system. In this case, Yaler acts as a secure "man in the middle", who handles two-way communication between your web client and your alarm system.

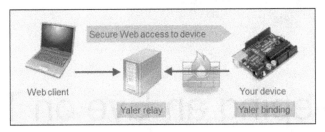

Yaler access

Installing YalerTunnel

The first step in installing YalerTunnel is to get a domain name. You can do this for free by going to www.yaler.net and following the instructions on the website.

On the BeagleBone:

1. Create a YalerTunnel directory:

   ```
   $ mkdir yalertunnel
   $ cd yalertunnel
   ```

2. Download the YalerTunnel source:

   ```
   $ curl -LO http://hg.yaler.org/yalertunnel2/downloads/
   YalerTunnel2.src.tar.gz
   ```

3. Unzip the source into the directory:

   ```
   $ tar xfzmv YalerTunnel2.src.tar.gz
   ```

4. Configure and create the code:

   ```
   $ ./configure && make
   ```

5. We can now enable either SSH or web access. If you want to have both web and SSH access, you will require two separate Yaler tunnels (domain names).

Enabling web access

In order to enable web access on your BeagleBone, you need to perform the following steps:

1. Download the `yalertunnel.service` startup script.

    ```
    $ curl -L http://yalertunnel.s3.amazonaws.com/yalertunnel.service
    -o /lib/systemd/system/yalertunnel.service
    ```

2. Create a symbolic link:

    ```
    $ ln -s  /lib/systemd/system/yalertunnel.service /etc/systemd/
    system/multi-user.target.wants/yalertunnel.service
    ```

3. Edit the script using the built in editor called Nano to set YOUR_RELAY_ DOMAIN, as well as the local IP (default: `localhost`), and port (default: `80`) of the local web service you want to make accessible via Yaler (to save your changes press *Ctrl* + *X*, then *Y*, and then *Enter*).

```
$ nano /lib/systemd/system/yalertunnel.service

[Unit]
Description=yalertunnel on port 80
ConditionPathExists=|/home/root/yalertunnel

[Service]
Working directory=/home/root/yalertunnel
ExecStart=/home/root/yalertunnel server localhost:80
    try.yaler.net:80 <YOUR_RELAY_DOMAIN> -min-listeners 4

[Install]
Wantedby=multi-user.target
```

4. Restart the BeagleBone to run the script:

    Now that we have enabled web access to the BeagleBone from an external source, one of the clever things we can do is serve a web page that has a link to a wireless hub. When you click on the link, you will be directed to the hub's login screen, just as if you had done this from your home network. Cool, huh?

    Here is a very simple example:

    ```
    <html>
      <head>
        <title>Wireless Hub Access Page</title>
      </head>
    ```

```
<body>
<h1>Here is a simple way of accessing your Router via
Yaler:</h1>


    <a href="http:192.168.10.1"> Here is my Router Page </a>

</body>
</html>
```

What you have to do is set up your socket server on the BeagleBone to serve this page instead of the standard /var/lib/cloud9/bone101/index.html page by renaming the original file index.html to index2.html, and then adding the above code as the new index.html.

The previously configured, simple web page looks like the following screenshot:

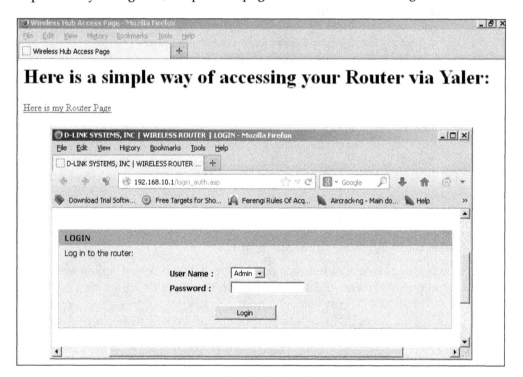

An example of a simple web page

You can now access your device from anywhere by simply entering http://<YOUR_RELAY_DOMAIN.yaler.net/ in your web browser.

For example, http://luke.skywalker.yaler.net/.

SSH access

It is also possible to access your BeagleBone with SSH (Secure Shell). A Secure Shell will allow you to run all sorts of terminal-based programs, such as Kismet for wireless device monitoring or Wireshark for network monitoring.

In order to install SSH access, we must perform the following steps:

1. Download the `yalertunnel-ssh.service` startup script:

   ```
   $ curl -L http://yalertunnel.s3.amazonaws.com/yalertunnel-ssh.
   service -o /lib/systemd/system/yalertunnel-ssh.service
   ```

2. Create a symbolic link:

   ```
   $ ln -s  /lib/systemd/system/yalertunnel-ssh.service /etc/systemd/
   system/multi-user.target.wants/yalertunnel-ssh.service
   ```

3. As with the web interface, we must edit the script to set YOUR_RELAY_DOMAIN, the local IP (default: `localhost`), and port (default: 22) of the local SSH service that you want to make accessible via Yaler.

   ```
   $ nano /lib/systemd/system/yalertunnel-ssh.service
   ```

   ```
   [Unit]
   Description=yalertunnel on port 22
   ConditionPathExists=|/home/root/yalertunnel


   [Service]
   WorkingDirectory=/home/root/yalertunnel
   ExecStart=/home/root/yalertunnel proxy localhost:22
     try.yaler.net:80
   <YOUR_RELAY_DOMAIN> -min-listners 8


   [Install]
   WantedBy=multi-user.target
   ```

4. Exit Nano and either reboot the system or type the following commands in the console.

5. Enter `systemctl --system daemon-reload`.

6. Then enter `systemctl start yalertunnel-ssh.service`.

Configuring PuTTY

Now that we have the firmware installed, it is time to access it using PuTTY. In order to do this, we must first configure PuTTY:

1. To start PuTTY, select the **Session** category and set the **Connection** type to **SSH**. Enter /<relay_domain> in **Host Name (or IP address)** and 22 in **Port**. For example, for my relay domain, williamprettysecurity-system1-ssh, the Host Name would be seen as in the following screenshot:

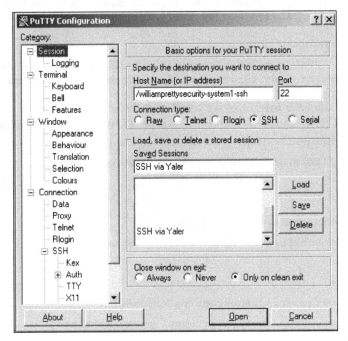

Session category

2. Select the **Connection** category and set **Seconds between keepalives (0 to turn off)** to 5.

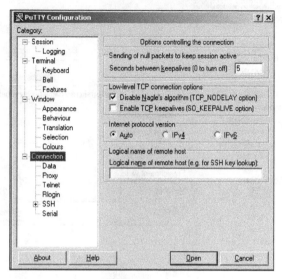

Connection category

3. Check the **Disable Nagle's algorithm (TCP_NODELAY option)** checkbox. (This will make the connection more responsible.)

4. Navigate to **Connection | Proxy** and set **Proxy type:** to **HTTP**. Enter try.yaler.net in **Proxy hostname** and 80 in **Port**.

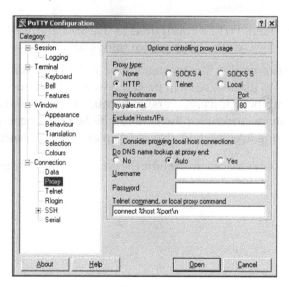

Proxy page

5. Navigate to **Connection | Data** and enter `root` in **Auto-login username**.

Data page

6. Select the **Session** category, enter a name such as `SSH via Yaler` in **Saved Sessions** and click **Save**.

7. Now that we have PuTTY configured to use SSH and we have established a YalerTunnel, let's see the kind of cool things we can do.

Well, first of all, we can hook a Bluetooth adapter and a WiFi adapter to our BeagleBone. In order to do this, we will need a powered USB hub. It is very important that the hub be a powered version because both the Bluetooth and WiFi adapters draw too much current for the USB on the BeagleBone to supply. While we are at it, the BeagleBone itself should also have an external 5V supply.

To use the Bluetooth adapter, we must edit the configuration file in `/var/lib/connman/settings`.

```
[global]
Timeservers=0.angstrom.pool.ntp.org;1.angstrom.pool.
ntp.org;2.angstrom.pool.ntp.org;3.angstrom.pool.ntp.org
OfflineMode=false

[Wired]
Enable=true

[WiFi]
Enable=true

[Bluetooth]
Enable=true <- Change this line from 'false' to 'true
```

This will enable Bluetooth devices on your BeagleBone; otherwise, the `hciconfig` `hci0` `up` command will give you an error.

The next thing that we have to do is install the WiFi tools package so that we can use the WiFi adapter.

You can do this with the following command:

```
opkg install wireless-tools
```

Reboot the system, and we are ready to try some wireless commands.

WiFi monitoring

You can see which wireless networks are active in your neighborhood. This is handy if you are monitoring an office environment for Rouge APs installed against the company's policy.

To do this, type the following code in the SSH terminal:

```
iwlist wlan0 scan
```

You will see the following code listing:

```
Cell 01 - Address: 00:11:22:33:44:55
          ESSID:"bills_network"
          Mode:Master
          Channel:11
          Frequency:2.462 GHz (Channel 11)
          Quality=100/100  Signal level:-47dBm  Noise level=- 100dBm
```

```
Encryption key:off
        .

        .

        .
```

You can see your wireless hub's link quality continuously on the screen by entering the following code:

```
watch -n 1 cat /proc/net/wireless
```

Or only once by entering the following code:

```
cat /proc/net/wireless
```

Wavemon

Wavemon is a simple ASCII text-based program that you can use to monitor your WiFi connections to the BeagleBone.

The software can be downloaded from

```
http://eden-feed.erg.abdn.ac.uk/wavemon/stable-releases/wavemon-
0.7.5.tar.bz2.
```

Once you install, configure, and make the software, you should see a screen much like the following screenshot:

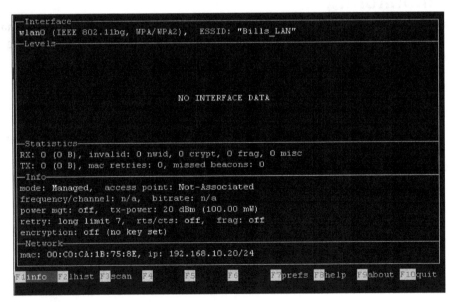

Wavemon screen

The following is a screen dump of the `ifconfig` command on my system:

```
root@beaglebone:~# ifconfig wlan0
wlan0     Link encap:Ethernet  HWaddr 00:C0:CA:1B:75:8E
          inet addr:192.168.10.20  Bcast:192.168.10.255
Mask:255.255.255.0
          UP BROADCAST MULTICAST  MTU:1500  Metric:1
          RX packets:0 errors:0 dropped:0 overruns:0 frame:0
          TX packets:0 errors:0 dropped:0 overruns:0 carrier:0
          collisions:0 txqueuelen:1000
          RX bytes:0 (0.0 B)  TX bytes:0 (0.0 B)
```

Bluetooth monitoring

Bluetooth monitoring can be done in much the same way as WiFi monitoring, with a few simple terminal commands.

To scan for Bluetooth devices within range, we use the `scan` command:

```
hcitool scan
Scanning ...
        00:60:57:10:29:50        Joe's 6310i
```

By running the previous command, we have found Joe's phone and now we can ask some basic questions:

```
root@beaglebone:~# hcitool  info  00:60:57:10:29:50
Requesting information ...
        BD Address:  00:60:57:10:29:50
        Device Name: Joe's 6310i
        LMP Version: 1.1 (0x1) LMP Subversion: 0x22c
        Manufacturer: Nokia Mobile Phones (1)
        Features: 0xbf 0x28 0x21 0x00 0x00 0x00 0x00 0x00
                <3-slot packets> <5-slot packets> <encryption> <slot
offset>
                <timing accuracy> <role switch> <sniff mode> <SCO link>
                <HV3 packets> <CVSD>
```

We can also "ping" Joe's phone (or any other Bluetooth device where we know the `bd_address`). This can come in handy if you want to know if your spouse or kids have arrived at home safely. Or, at least their phone has!

We can do this using the `l2ping` command:

```
root@beaglebone:~# l2ping 00:60:57:10:29:50
Ping: 00:60:57:10:29:50 from 00:18:F8:89:A3:F6 (data size 44) ...
0 bytes from 00:60:57:10:29:50 id 0 time 64.50ms
0 bytes from 00:60:57:10:29:50 id 1 time 13.40ms
0 bytes from 00:60:57:10:29:50 id 2 time 15.84ms
0 bytes from 00:60:57:10:29:50 id 3 time 13.40ms
0 bytes from 00:60:57:10:29:50 id 4 time 15.72ms
0 bytes from 00:60:57:10:29:50 id 5 time 14.48ms
0 bytes from 00:60:57:10:29:50 id 6 time 13.52ms
0 bytes from 00:60:57:10:29:50 id 7 time 13.95ms
0 bytes from 00:60:57:10:29:50 id 8 time 16.66ms
0 bytes from 00:60:57:10:29:50 id 9 time 13.85ms
10 sent, 10 received, 0% loss
```

In order to find out the `bd_address` of your family member's phone, you can simply scan for it sometime when you know that they are at home and in range.

Summary

In this chapter we learned how to install and use some basic Linux commands to monitor wireless devices in proximity to our alarm system. We also installed a simple WiFi monitoring software package.

Many of you are probably wondering why I didn't use common packages such as Kismet or Aircrack. That is because there are already a number of good online tutorials about how to install these packages. Also, the purpose of these packages, Aircrack in particular, is not so much that of an intrusion detection (ID) system as just penetration testing.

My search on the Web turned up a number of wireless and wired intrusion detection packages. Unfortunately, they were either intended for X86-based systems or another Linux package distribution such as Ubuntu or Debian.

In the next chapter we will look at just some of the many more cool things you can do with your system, now that you have it up and running.

9
Going Further

Well, you made it this far. So, if you built the hardware and the software in the previous chapters, and had your new best friend (the carpenter) help you with the installation, then you are well on your way to having a terrific integrated security system.

So where do we go from here?

Well, here are a few suggestions to make your system even better.

In this chapter, we will see some additional devices and sensors that can be added to your system. Most of these devices connect to the BeagleBone through USB interfaces and speak ASCII.

An RFID reader

You can easily build an RFID reader using parts available from **SparkFun** electronics.

The carrier board connects to the BeagleBone through a USB cable, and will be seen by the operating system as a simple serial device.

RFID reader (image is CC BY-NC-SA 3.0)

You plug your RFID module into the board, and when an RFID device is passed by the reader, the serial number is sent to the BeagleBone through USB, through the ASCII text. All you need to do now is look up the serial number in a database, either on the BeagleBone or a host computer, and if required, grant access to the location.

A fingerprint scanner

You can also add a fingerprint scanner relatively easily.

Fingerprint scanner (images are CC BY-NC-SA 3.0)

The scanner once again plugs into a USB port. It does require a fair amount of software to control, but most of the actual reading and whatnot is handled by the fingerprint module. What you have to do is add prints to a database in a setup mode and scan for them on an operate mode. This device requires a USB-to-TTL adapter, in order to connect to the BeagleBone in the same manner as the other devices. SparkFun sells several versions of these adapters.

A geophone sensor

A geophone is a device that detects low frequency vibrations, like footsteps or a vehicle passing.

Geophone element (images are CC BY-NC-SA 3.0)

If you live in an area with heavy vehicle traffic, this project may not be for you.

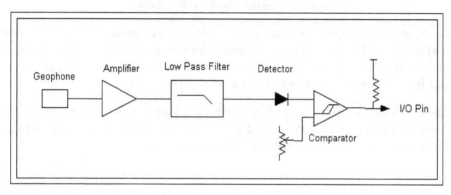

Geophone detector block diagram

The previous figure shows the block diagram of a geophone sensor. What we do is we take the analog signal that comes from the geophone and amplify it so that we can detect footsteps. Then we pass it through a low-pass filter, which removes any high frequencies that might have gotten into the signal. We then pass this analog signal to a detector, which gives us a DC level that corresponds to the amplified level of the signal from the geophone. We compare this DC level to a preset level (think of this as a sensitivity adjustment) and connect the output of the comparator to an I/O pin of the BeagleBone.

Now we can detect footsteps in the vicinity of our home or business.

A barcode scanner

Barcode scanner (images are CC BY-NC-SA 3.0)

Another simple input device is a barcode scanner. Once again it should look like a **usbserial** device to Linux. The scanner sends the ASCII text to the BeagleBone, as if it was coming from a keyboard. So now you can scan vehicles, boxes and so on coming into your home or business, using either a barcode or an RFID tag, or both.

All of these devices, with the exception of the geophone, require a USB connection. What I would suggest is a POWERED 4-port USB hub connected to your BeagleBone, and your various sensors and wireless devices connected to it.

Right now, BeagleBone is powered by a 5V USB.

If you want to connect devices to the USB on the BeagleBone, you should either use a powered USB hub or an external power to the BeagleBone, or both.

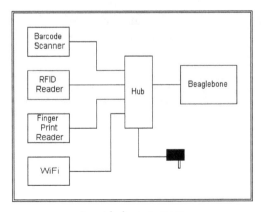

4-port hub connections

Summary

Hopefully this book and this chapter have inspired you to create your own high-tech alarm system.

I am sure that in the future, others will take what I have started here and build on it. At least I hope so.

In the meantime, stay safe; have fun building a home security system with BeagleBone! The following are the links to the CAD software that has been used here. It is a freeware, and you will need ExpressPCB to read the schematic and PCB files.

PCB software: http://www.expresspcb.com/ExpressPCBHtm/Download.htm

Assembly diagrams: http://fritzing.org/download/

The following kits are available from SparkFun Electronics Inc on this link

www.sparkfun.com.

- RFID starter kit: RTL-11839
- Fingerprint scanner: SEN-11792
- Geophone: SEN-11744
- Barcode scanner: SEN-09166
- Serial to USB: BOB-00718

Index

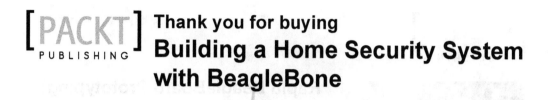

Thank you for buying
Building a Home Security System with BeagleBone

About Packt Publishing

Packt, pronounced 'packed', published its first book "*Mastering phpMyAdmin for Effective MySQL Management*" in April 2004 and subsequently continued to specialize in publishing highly focused books on specific technologies and solutions.

Our books and publications share the experiences of your fellow IT professionals in adapting and customizing today's systems, applications, and frameworks. Our solution based books give you the knowledge and power to customize the software and technologies you're using to get the job done. Packt books are more specific and less general than the IT books you have seen in the past. Our unique business model allows us to bring you more focused information, giving you more of what you need to know, and less of what you don't.

Packt is a modern, yet unique publishing company, which focuses on producing quality, cutting-edge books for communities of developers, administrators, and newbies alike. For more information, please visit our website: www.packtpub.com.

Writing for Packt

We welcome all inquiries from people who are interested in authoring. Book proposals should be sent to author@packtpub.com. If your book idea is still at an early stage and you would like to discuss it first before writing a formal book proposal, contact us; one of our commissioning editors will get in touch with you.

We're not just looking for published authors; if you have strong technical skills but no writing experience, our experienced editors can help you develop a writing career, or simply get some additional reward for your expertise.

Raspberry Pi Super Cluster

ISBN: 978-1-78328-619-5   Paperback: 126 pages

Build your own parallel-computing cluster using Raspberry Pi in the comfort of your home

1. Learn about parallel computing by building your own system using Raspberry Pi

2. Build a two-node parallel computing cluster

3. Integrate Raspberry Pi with Hadoop to build your own super cluster

Raspberry Pi Home Automation with Arduino

ISBN: 978-1-84969-586-2   Paperback: 176 pages

Automate your home with a set of exciting projects for the Raspberry Pi!

1. Learn how to dynamically adjust your living environment with detailed step-by-step examples

2. Discover how you can utilize the combined power of the Raspberry Pi and Arduino for your own projects

3. Revolutionize the way you interact with your home on a daily basis

Please check **www.PacktPub.com** for information on our titles